The Laws of Increase
Developing a Sower's Heart

Larry Stockstill

Bethany World Prayer Center
Baker, Louisiana

xulon
PRESS

Copyright © 2004 by Larry Stockstill

The Laws of Increase
by Larry Stockstill

Printed in the United States of America

ISBN 1-594678-71-5

All rights reserved solely by the author. The author guarantees all contents are original and do not infringe upon the legal rights of any other person or work. No part of this book may be reproduced in any form without the permission of the author. The views expressed in this book are not necessarily those of the publisher.

Unless otherwise indicated, Bible quotations are taken from the King James Version of the Bible.

www.xulonpress.com

Contents

Chapter 1 The Sacrifice of Increase 7

Sacrificial Giving: Planting the Seed 9
Sacrificial "Dying": Relinquishing the Seed 12
Sacrificial Living: Reaping the Harvest
  of the Seed...14
Sacrificial Tithing: Giving Ten Percent of Your Income
  as Seed 16
Sacrificial Offerings: Giving Seed Above
  the Tithe 18
Sacrificial Planting: Scattering the Seed.....................20
Sacrificial Sowing: Planting Abundant Seed 23

Chapter 2 The Offering of Increase 27

Offerings as Worship 29
Offerings as Seed 35

Offerings as Investment 39
Offerings to Reap Souls 41

Chapter 3 Waiting for Increase 47

Patience for the Harvest 48
Lessons of Waiting 51
    The Testing of Your Heart 52
    The Testing of Your Faithfulness 57
    The Testing of Your Patience 63

Chapter 4 Expecting the Increase 67

Expect to Receive Vision 70
Expect to Receive Seed 78
Expect a Harvest 82

Chapter 5 Receiving Your Increase 89

You Must Conceive Before You Can Receive 94
Be It Done According to Your Word 103
There Shall Be a Performance 105

CHAPTER 1

The Sacrifice of Increase

Everybody wants more! Babies demand more milk, mothers crave more time, fathers strive to make more money for their families, and churches come up with elaborate schemes to attract more members. It seems an inescapable part of life to want more. This desire for more, however, is not necessarily bad; in fact, God wants to give us more in every area of life. The problem is that we don't know how to receive that increase. We are ignorant of the laws that God has put in place to bless and increase us.

That's what I want to share with you in this book—how to increase in your life until you are living in the abundance that God intended for you. I want to teach you the spiritual laws that govern your ability to increase, and I want to show you how you can live that superabundant, overflowing life that is yours as a child of God.

If we take the word *sower* and use it as an acronym, we can discover five basic laws of increase. S-O-W-E-R—five little letters that stand for five big principles in the kingdom of God.

The first letter is "S," and that stands for the word *sacrifice*. If we want God to bless us, we are going to have to be willing to sacrifice. Sacrifice is the opposite of greed, and God can never bless greediness. The world, however, is full of greed. People want to get rich quick, playing the lottery or gambling on the casino boats. For people like that, money is their god; it's their life. All they think about is getting more money one way or another.

People can be broke, without a cent to their names, and still be full of the love of money. It's the attitude of the heart that counts. God isn't concerned with the amount you have or don't have—He wants to be sure that what you have does not have you! He wants to know that you love Him, not money.

Psalm 115:14 says, "The Lord shall increase you more and more, you and your children." God desires to bless and increase you, but before He can do so, you have got to be delivered from the love of money. You've got to say, "Lord, I don't care what I have on this earth. I'm just a pilgrim passing through this life, on my way to my home in heaven. Whatever you give me on the journey, I'll be a good steward of it. I won't hold on to it and grasp it tightly. I won't let it make me proud or cause me to exalt myself over others. I'm just a channel of blessing with whatever you choose to give me." That's the sower's heart!

God wants you to be a sower all the days of your life, caring about others and meeting their needs with the resources you have. I've been in nations of the world where people live in stick houses covered with burlap. Compared to what they have, the worst slum in the United States is a paradise. In this country, even the poorest of us have more than most people around the world. We are indeed blessed, and with that blessing comes the privilege of sacrifice.

Sacrificial Giving: Planting the Seed

Sacrifice—that's the first principle of the laws of increase. A sower in the kingdom of God is a person of sacrifice, someone who will plant a seed in the lives of others. Some people, however, are so tightfisted that they don't want to part with even a seed, not realizing the immense potential of blessing within that seed if they will but release it.

A seed of corn by itself can't do you one bit of good. It can't satisfy your appetite at all. If you eat one little seed at 7:00 in the morning, it won't even last you until 8:00! There's just not enough in it to nourish you in any way. But if you take that little seed and plant it, it can produce thousands upon thousands of kernels. You'll have enough to eat your fill and plenty left over to bless others with—all because you planted one tiny seed.

God has given certain laws of increase, and giving sacrificially through planting a seed is the first. I've learned over the years that when a church or an individual gives faithfully to world missions, God increases them more and more. That's what we've done at Bethany. Every year since the church began, we have increased our giving to missions. Every year we sow more and more seed, and every year God increases us more and more. Not only does He meet all our needs, but He also blesses us with an increasing store of seed to sow. This past year, 2003, we have been privileged to give nearly $3 million to both local and world missions. To God be all the glory!

When we talk about sowing seed, most of us think of a financial seed. That's one kind of seed, and God does want to increase you financially. But He also wants to increase you more and more in the souls you reap and the gifts of the Spirit that you develop. He wants to give you a sower's mentality so you will increase in every area in your life. Just think about it: more finances, more souls, more grace, more peace, more joy, more love! God is longing to give all that and more to you, if you will learn the secret of sacrificial giving.

A seed is God's potential miracle. Within it is life, and when it's planted, increase comes. In Luke 5 we see how Jesus, the greatest sower of all, reaped souls into the kingdom of God. In this chapter of the Scriptures, we find Simon Peter washing his net and disinterested in the Gospel. He was just going about his business, doing what he did every day. People all around him had gathered to hear Jesus, but Simon was not one of them. He was just standing there on the shore, washing his net. So Jesus went to him. Isn't that interesting? He wouldn't go to Jesus, so Jesus went to him. Jesus got into Simon's boat, and then He sat down. In other words, if you want to reap lost souls, you've got to go to them and "get into their boat." That's what Jesus did.

The lost are all around us; you don't have to look far to find a lost person. Our college campuses, for example, are full of international students who would love to be befriended by an American. Did you know that the two

The Laws of Increase

Japanese men who launched the attack on Pearl Harbor had both been students in the United States? Who knows if the future might have been different had someone made an effort to get into their boat while they were in our country?

A few years ago, the Lord gave me the opportunity to use this principle of sacrificial giving to minister friendship to an international student at LSU. I was waiting for my daughter in the lobby of a building where she was having a harp lesson. I had my two young sons with me and was trying to keep them entertained while Melissa finished the lesson. As we waited, a young man came in and walked over to a pay phone. He made his call and began speaking in a language that was not English. One of my little boys listened intently, and when the young man finished his conversation, my son went up to him and asked, "Who are you talking to?" You know, children are not afraid to get into someone's boat!

Anyway, I went up to this man, who looked like he was of Middle Eastern descent, and began talking to him. I found out he was an accomplished cellist and had been studying his instrument for eleven years. He told me he was from Turkey, and we exchanged phone numbers. A couple of days later he called me, and I made arrangements to take his girlfriend and him out to eat. My family and I brought them to a Lebanese restaurant where they could get food similar to what they had back home. Oh, but they enjoyed themselves! They ate and ate and were just so happy to find a place that served such food.

I didn't tell them I was a pastor; I didn't witness to them with words; I just sat down in their boat with them. I simply sacrificed a little bit of time in order to be with them and get to know them. That's the way to begin sacrificially sowing into the lives of those who don't know the Lord. Take an interest in them. Spend time with them. Just get into their boat!

Sacrificial "Dying": Relinquishing the Seed

John 12:24 says, "Verily, verily, I say unto you, except a corn of wheat fall into the ground and die, it abideth alone: but if it die, it bringeth forth much fruit." Your seed, before it can produce anything, has to die. As long as you have control over that seed, it cannot multiply. But when you take a seed, be it an act of love or a witness for Jesus or a financial gift, and you give it up and plant it in the ground, it will bring forth much fruit. The "life" that comes from the seed follows the "death" of the seed. It's one of the great paradoxes of the Bible: If you want to live, you've got to die. That means you die to whatever it is you are planting. You make it useless to you. It's inoperative in your life, and you relinquish all control of it.

Sometimes people give with the idea of what they're going to get back. They are always looking at the benefit they will reap. However, godly sowing means something dies. Yes, God will bless your giving, but you're missing the whole point of what it means to be a sower if you're always looking for what you're going to get back. A sower gives sacrificially—no strings attached, no demands made, and all control of the seed surrendered.

Now notice verse 25 of John 12: "He that loveth his life

shall lose it; and he that hateth his life in this world shall keep it unto life eternal." There it is again—that paradox, or seeming contradiction. It's the principle of sacrifice, the willful putting to death of something dear to you. In the Old Testament, when Araunah offered David whatever he needed to present an offering to the Lord, David refused, saying he would not offer to the Lord a sacrifice that cost him nothing (2 Sam. 24:24). David knew that by its very nature, a sacrifice had to cost something. If it costs nothing, it isn't really a sacrifice.

In Genesis 4, we read the first account of a sacrifice. Abel offered to God something that was precious to him: several of his best lambs. His brother Cain, on the other hand, also brought a sacrifice, but it was not something dear to him—just a lot of vegetables! The Bible says in verse 4 that God accepted Abel's sacrifice, but not Cain's. We know from other portions of Scripture that when God was pleased with a sacrifice, He literally sent fire from heaven and consumed it; if He was not pleased, He didn't send the fire. In those days, you could tell pretty easily if God was pleased with a sacrifice!

Can't you just imagine the scene? With a mighty whoosh, fire came down from heaven and consumed Abel's sacrifice, and Cain was just sitting there, watching and waiting for the fire to burn up his sacrifice. But the fire never came, because God did not accept Cain's halfhearted sacrifice. And Cain was offended. Not only was he offended, but he also resented Abel for having his sacrifice accepted. You know the rest of the story. Consumed with jealousy, Cain plotted and killed his brother—all because of a sacrifice.

Sacrificial Living: Reaping the Harvest of the Seed

Now let's look at sacrifice in the New Testament. Philippians 4:14-15 says, "Notwithstanding ye have well done, that ye did communicate with my affliction. Now ye Philippians know also, that in the beginning of the gospel, when I departed from Macedonia, no church communicated with me as concerning giving and receiving, but ye only." Paul was a missionary, and he knew what it was like to live from the sacrifices of others. Verse 15 tells us the Philippian church was the only church that supported Paul when he went from Macedonia. Not only did they send him an offering at that time, but also when he was in Thessalonica, they sent help to him more than once (v. 16). Although Paul had established other churches, the Philippian church alone supported him in his missionary endeavors. They knew how to be sowers in the kingdom of God.

Now notice the seventeenth verse: "Not because I desire a gift: but I desire fruit that may abound to your account." Paul cared more about the eternal reward the Philippians would receive for helping him than he did about receiving the actual gift. That's an important point to remember because the devil will tell you that the only reason pastors ever teach on giving or increase is because they're trying to get money from you. That's a lie, and you need to recognize it as such.

Don't let the devil steal your blessing from you. Most pastors I know live very sacrificially. Many of them have given up good-paying jobs in the secular world to serve

God's people. We've got men like that on our staff. They're not interested in trying to get your money; they just want to bless and help you.

Most of you probably have a bank account. You deposit money into it and watch it increase. In the same way, you also have a heavenly account. When you sow a financial gift into the kingdom of God, you are making a deposit into that heavenly account. You are storing up treasure for eternity, with a value far greater than any earthly possession.

Right before verse 17 in Philippians 4, in verses 11–13, Paul said that it really didn't matter if he had a little or a lot. He had lived both ways, but he knew that no matter his circumstances, God would give him the strength to do whatever he had to do. He just wanted the Philippians to have fruit to their account, a heavenly reward for sowing a seed into the kingdom of God.

Like Paul, I can say that I'm not interested in getting your money. God will provide for our needs as a church one way or another. He always has, and He always will. No person is our source; only God has the right to be that. But as a pastor, I do want to see every person in my church with a heavenly account that is increasing more and more. I want to see each one of them blessed beyond measure as they live sacrificially, planting the seed in the kingdom of God. I want all of them to be able to look back at the end of a year and say, "Look what the Lord has done! Look at how I've been blessed. Look at how my finances have prospered and how I've increased." Blessings on earth and eternal treasures in heaven—that's what awaits those who will live sacrificially for the cause of Christ.

Sacrificial Tithing:
Giving Ten Percent of Your Income as Seed

If you desire to open your heavenly account, you've got to start with tithing, or giving 10 percent of your income to the Lord. That's the first step. When you begin to tithe, you step out from under the curse. As Malachi 3:9–10 says, "Ye are cursed with a curse: for ye have robbed me, even this whole nation. Bring ye all the tithes into the storehouse . . . [and I will] pour you out a blessing, that there shall not be room enough to receive it." The tithe belongs to God, so when you keep it for yourself, you are actually stealing from Him. When you give Him the tithe, however, you are really just giving back to Him what is His already. Then God, in turn, will "rebuke the devourer" (v. 11) for you, protecting your source of income.

The devil wants to cut off your income; he wants to steal from you everything he can. When you don't tithe, you're under a curse, and the devil has every legal right to steal from you. That's why when I get paid, the first thing I do is tithe. I don't wait until the end of the month or just whenever I get around to it. No, it's important—I want the blessing and protection of God over my family and me, so I give the tithe immediately. Treating the tithe carelessly is like going to the mall, getting out of your car, and leaving the engine running and the doors wide open. You're just asking for trouble. You're practically begging somebody to steal your car! In the same way, if you don't tithe, you're saying, in effect, "Here you go, devil. Take whatever you want." Now that's a dangerous position for anyone!

The Laws of Increase

I've discovered the protection that comes from tithing, and many other people have, too. One of the most impressive stories I ever read about the protection that comes from tithing is the story of Alexander Kerr, the founder of the company that makes Kerr canning jars. Mr. Kerr's company was located in San Francisco, and in the early part of the twentieth century, there was a huge earthquake there, followed by a devastating fire. Mr. Kerr was not in San Francisco when the earthquake struck and could not immediately find out what had happened to his glass factory. Think about it: a glass factory right in the middle of an area that had just been through an earthquake. After a few days he received a telegram saying that in addition to the earthquake, there was now a fire raging through the city. The senders of the telegram said they couldn't get to the factory, but they were sure it was destroyed because the entire city lay in ruins.

Now Mr. Kerr was a tither, and when he got the news, he refused to believe that his factory was gone. He insisted that God would protect his factory, because he was a tither and that factory was his source of income. A week later he got another telegram from the same people who had sent him the first one. They amazedly told him to return to the city and see the wondrous thing God had done. Within a mile and a half in every direction of the Kerr glass factory, every other building was leveled by fire. But the Kerr building, constructed of wood and surrounded by a wooden fence, was unscathed. The fire had come up to the fence, and then it was as though it had jumped over the factory. Not one board of the factory was burned! Just as amazing was the fact that not one glass jar in the factory was broken. Not even one jar was cracked, though the factory had gone through the earthquake with the rest of the city!

Mr. Kerr was so blessed and so grateful that he wrote a tract called *The Cure for Poverty,* in which he explained how tithing had protected his source of income. He followed this a little later with another tract, *God's Loving Money Rule for Your Financial Prosperity.* From that point on, he inserted one of these two tracts into every case of canning jars made, and by the time he died in 1924, he had distributed over five million of them (Ken C. Kemble, editor, "I Will Rebuke the Devourer," *The Alethia Herald,* n.d., <http://www.kinship-ministries.org/Publications/Rebuke.htm.> December 12, 2003). So you see, it pays to tithe!

Sacrificial Offerings: Giving Seed Above the Tithe

The tithe is owed to the Lord; it's not ours to begin with. Offerings, however, are something we give to the Lord above the tithe. It can be a missionary offering, like the one the Philippians gave to Paul. Look at what the Lord says about these kinds of offerings. They are "an odor of a sweet smell, a sacrifice acceptable, well-pleasing to God" (Phil. 4:18). When you sow into the Lord's work, it smells like a sweet perfume to Him. He regards it as an acceptable sacrifice, and He is pleased with you for giving it. Now go on to verse 19 and read the punch line: "But my God shall supply all your need according to his riches in glory by Christ Jesus."

How many of your needs does it say that God will

supply? All of them! And according to what does He supply your needs? Is it according to the economy or your salary? No, it's according to *His* riches. And where are those riches? In heaven! God already has all that you need and is just waiting to give it to you. That's something to shout about it!

When we give offerings, there is a supernatural release of finances in heaven. But first we have to give up something, plant the seed, and let it die before God can meet our needs. This point was really brought home to me one Thanksgiving. A woman in the church brought me a fried turkey for the holiday. In fact, the Lord directed her to buy four turkeys, fry them, and give them to four different people. She really didn't have any extra money to do it, but she just went ahead and did it anyway. She bought the turkeys, and then she got a call from her mortgage company, telling her she had overpaid her insurance and would be receiving a check for $390!

This woman had learned the principle of sacrificial giving. The year before, she had taken $70 and bought Christmas presents for children whose fathers were in prison. Again, she didn't have the money, and again, God honored her giving. A few days after she had purchased the gifts, she heard from a company that had bricked her home for her two years earlier. The auditor was going over the books and found out that they owed her $70! She got back every penny she had given away. Her offerings were, indeed, a sweet fragrance to the Lord.

Hebrews 13:15 teaches us another principle of the sacrifice of increase: "By him therefore let us offer the sacrifice of praise to God continually, that is, the fruit of our lips giving thanks to his name." When you offer God the sacrifice of praise—that means praising Him even when you don't feel like it—the "fire" comes down upon you and God accepts it as a pleasing sacrifice to Him. Verse 16 continues, "But to do good and to communicate forget not: for with such sacrifices God is well pleased." I like the way the NIV says it: "And do not forget to do good *and to share with others,* for with such sacrifices God is pleased" (italics added). God wants you to share with others. He knows that it's a sacrifice for you, but He is well pleased when you do it. I don't know about you, but I want to please God, so I'm going to be a "praiser" and a giver, sacrificing what I have to God and others.

Sacrificial Planting: Scattering the Seed

Once we've decided to make a sacrifice to God, releasing our seed without thought of recompense, it's time to actually plant it. Proverbs 11:24 tells us how to do it: "There is that scattereth, and yet increaseth; and there is that withholdeth more than is meet, but it tendeth to poverty." Notice the word *scatter*. We're to scatter our seed, that is, to release it with abandon.

In Bible times, they did not plant their seed one grain at a time. They didn't do it like we do when we go into our backyard and plant a garden. We dig our hole, drop in a seed, move over twelve inches or so, dig another hole, drop in another seed, and on we go. In the days of the Bible, however, they scattered seed for sowing. They just walked along and threw it out. It was just like Jesus described in the parable of the sower: some of the seed fell on the wayside, some fell on stony soil, some fell on thorny ground, and some fell on good ground. But the sower just sowed the seed then let it grow and develop on its own. He didn't watch the seed and worry about it, he didn't go looking to see where the seed had fallen, and he wasn't stingy in sowing it.

A lot of people have a problem with this concept. You might be thinking, "If I reach down into my 90 percent that I have over and above the tithe, and I take an offering and just scatter it, I'll never get blessed." But that's not what the Word of God says. In our verse in Proverbs it says that the one that scatters actually increases, and the one who is stingy and withholds his seed becomes poor! Isn't that amazing? It's another one of those paradoxes in the Bible. If you want to live, you have to die; and if you want to increase, you have to scatter your seed.

Now go on to verse 25 of Proverbs 11: "The liberal soul shall be made fat: and he that watereth shall be watered also himself." The generous person is going to get fat! Not weight wise, of course, but fat in spirit, abounding and increasing more and more. And when you water others, you'll be watered, too, when you're dry. It's a principle of Scripture: You reap what you sow. If you sow abundantly, you reap abundantly, and if you sow sparingly, you reap sparingly.

To scatter your seed means to generously, liberally sow it. It's not a stingy little miserly drop here and there. It's almost a reckless abandon to giving. It's like Ecclesiastes

11:1 says, "Cast thy bread upon the waters: for thou shalt find it after many days." The verse doesn't say to sit there and wait for your ship to come in. It emphatically says, "Cast!" That means scatter your bread upon the waters, and afterwards, you'll find it again. It's going to come back to you. You are going to be blessed because no matter how much you give, you can never out give God.

As a pastor, I've learned that lesson and seen it work in our church. From the very beginning, we purposed to scatter our seed abroad in world missions, and every year we have increased the amount we give. It seems the more we give, the more God blesses us. That's why I'm not afraid each year to just go ahead and increase our missions budget. We give in many, many different areas, scattering our seed here and there, but God always brings it back to us.

Verse 4 in Ecclesiastes 11 says, "He that observeth the wind shall not sow; and he that regardeth the clouds shall not reap." You can't look at the economy and decide what you're going to sow based on that. You can't look at your checkbook, either, and base your giving on that. You have to listen to the Holy Spirit.

When we built our $2½ million sanctuary at the north campus in 1985, I remember thinking we would need every penny we could get to have the necessary funds for building. As I was praying, I felt the Lord was saying to me, "Increase your giving to missions, and I will make it up to you in construction costs." We increased our giving to missions, and the Lord did just what He said He would. One of our pastors came on staff about that time, and because of his design and supervision, we saved $300,000 in architect fees. That's the way it's been in our church time and time again.

"In the morning sow thy seed, and in the evening withhold not thine hand: for thou knowest not whether shall prosper, either this or that, or whether they both shall be alike good" (Eccles. 11:6). Don't try to stop and analyze everything anytime you're even thinking about sowing. If you do, you'll never do anything; you'll talk yourself out of giving if you try to figure it all out. Just sow the seed! Throw it out there—in the morning, in the evening, whenever and wherever the Holy Spirit leads. You might not know which seed will prosper, but He does and He will lead you.

Sacrificial Sowing: Planting Abundant Seed

In 2 Corinthians 9:6 we gain another insight on sowing. First, we purpose to make the sacrifice; then, we scatter our seed; and finally, we do it abundantly. The verse reads, "But this I say, He which soweth sparingly shall reap also sparingly; and he which soweth bountifully shall reap also bountifully." That means if you plant two tomato seeds, you're going to get maybe eighteen tomatoes; but if you sow a thousand tomato seeds, you're going to reap a harvest of thousands of tomatoes. The size of your harvest is up to you. God will bless any seed you sow, whether it's small or large, but the more you sow, the more you're going to reap.

Some people say, "Well, if God wants to bless me, He'll just go ahead and do it when He's ready." No, God will bless you when *you* get good and ready for it. He wants to bless you, but you've got to plant that seed first. As long as you're holding it in your fist, it can't do you any good.

Galatians 6:7 makes it perfectly clear: "Be not deceived; God is not mocked: for whatsoever a man soweth, that shall he also reap."

Verse 7 of 2 Corinthians 9 further says that we must not give grudgingly or out of duty, but from our heart, cheerfully as we have purposed to do. The word *grudgingly* means "sorrowfully." So when you give a missionary offering, don't take out your handkerchief and wipe your face all the way to the offering bucket, crying about what you're giving up. And don't give out of duty, either. Don't walk up to that offering bucket with teeth clenched, saying, "I'll do it, but I sure don't want to." That's not the kind of offering God wants.

God wants you to give cheerfully; in fact, He loves a cheerful giver. The word in the Greek for this kind of giving is translated "hilarious." That's the kind of offering that pleases Him—an offering that laughs hilariously all the way to the offering bucket! Your attitude is everything. I've noticed that people who are liberal and generous are people of faith. They believe that if they give, it will be given back to them. You know the verse: "good measure, pressed down, and shaken together" (Luke 6:38). That's what generous people have discovered. They know that if they use a teaspoon on God, He'll use a teaspoon on them; but if they use a dump truck on Him, that's what He's going to use in return.

This principle of sacrificial, cheerful giving has nothing to do with the amount you give. God knows your financial condition, and He knows you can't give what you don't have. Remember the story of the widow's mite? Jesus said she gave more than all the others because she gave all she had, even though it was a very small amount.

It's all relative. What might be a sacrifice for me to give might not be anything to you, or vice versa. But one thing I know is it's not a sacrifice until it bleeds. It's got to cost you something. God sees everything you do. He takes notice when you give up that bass boat you wanted and sow the seed into Bibles for China instead. He knows how much you wanted that new television but gave the money to a missionary instead. God is not ignorant of your actions, and He will reward you accordingly.

Sometimes God provides us with unexpected income that we can use as seed. But what do most of us do? We eat the seed! We don't even recognize it as our opportunity to sow. When you receive an unexpected blessing, however, scatter that seed. Start giving to a missionary or someone you know that is in need. God is surely watching.

I like the way the Amplified Bible reads in 2 Corinthians 9:7. It says, ". . . not grudgingly or of necessity, for God loveth, and takes pleasure in, and prizes above other things, and is unwilling to abandon or do without, a cheerful giver." He's unwilling to abandon a cheerful giver! Look at Jacob in the Old Testament. When he fled from Israel, he left with nothing but a stick in his hand. After he saw his vision of the ladder going up to heaven, he became a tither. He did that for twenty years, and when he returned, he had so much increase that he sent herds of cattle and all kinds of gifts ahead to his brother Esau. He told the Lord, "With my staff I passed over this Jordan, and now I am become two bands" (Gen. 32:10).

God wants to increase you. He wants your car to be paid for, and He doesn't want it breaking down all the time. He wants your children to have food and clothing and all that they need. He wants to bless you so much that you lift up your eyes on the vast harvest fields of the world and desire to sow your seed there. Today, start giving your sacrifice to the Lord, and He will increase you more and more!

CHAPTER 2

The Offering of Increase

Now that we've learned about sacrifice as the first component in the laws of increase, we're ready to move on to the second letter in our acronym of SOWER. The "S" stands for sacrifice, and the "O" stands for offering. We've already talked about sacrifice and its role in bringing increase in our lives. We know that giving the tithe is a sacrifice that is required of us. All of us, I'm sure, could find other ways to spend our money, but when we give the tithe, we are giving back to God what is rightfully His anyway. We owe Him the tithe.

When we talk about offerings, however, we are moving into a level that is beyond and above the tithe. Thank God for the tithe and all those who are faithfully giving in that way to the kingdom of God. But, brothers and sisters, the tithe is really just the beginning point for the person who wants to be a sower in God's work. A true sower not only sacrificially gives of his income through the tithe, but he also gives offerings above the tithe.

I know some of you will have a hard time with this. You're thinking, "Isn't the tithe enough? If I have to give offerings, where's it going to end?" I'll tell you where it will end—"The Lord shall increase you more and more, you and your children" (Ps. 115:14). As you move to a higher level of giving, the Lord gives you a higher level of increase. It's really that simple!

Sacrifice deals primarily with that which is required of us. The many sacrifices in the Old Testament were required of the people. Given to God out of a sense of obligation, a sacrifice was always an intentional thing, a duty to be performed. That pretty much sums up the tithe and its role in our lives. Ten percent of our income belongs to the Lord. We respect it as something holy and make sure to give it to the Lord, and He in turn protects our source of income and rebukes the devourer from our lives.

I recently read an almost unbelievable story about a man named Perry Hayden, who, along with some other people, decided to experiment with the tithe. In September 1940, he planted one cubic inch of wheat seed (360 kernels), with the intention of tithing from the harvest. The seed was planted and yielded a harvest of 50 cubic inches in 1941. As planned, they tithed to the local church and planted the increase, which was 45 cubic inches of seed. In 1942, their yield was 70 pounds of wheat, from which they gave 7 pounds as their tithe and planted the remaining 63 pounds. By this point, news of the experiment was spreading, and great interest in the tithing project was generated. The harvest continued increasing exponentially each year until 1945, the sixth and final year of the experiment. The yield was now so great that they no longer had enough property on which to plant the seed. So they divided the seed among a number of local farmers, all of whom promised to tithe on the increase. In 1946 the harvest of these men reached 72,150 bushels of wheat.

The local miller had kept track of the yields of other farmers in the area and compared them to the tithing farmers. Based on the state averages for each year of production, the miller estimated that if the tithing farmers had planted the full harvest each year, they would have come out with a total yield of 5,297 bushels. In actuality, they had planted 90 percent of the harvest each year (keeping out 10 percent as a tithe) and had ended with a total yield of 72,150 bushels (David McArthur, *The Intelligent Heart,* n.d., <http://www.virtualresourcelibrary.org/fundraising.htm>, December 12, 2003).

Those men were not hindered one bit by the amount that they tithed. They just kept increasing more and more each year until they could not contain it. The principle is the same for us. The tithe does not take anything away from us, but rather it releases the first principle of increase in our lives. It opens the windows of heaven to us so that the blessings and abundance of God can flow into our lives (Mal. 3:10). If the windows are closed, nothing can flow from God to us, but when we give the tithe, we open the very windows of heaven on our behalf.

Offerings as Worship

The tithe is felt equally by all who participate in giving it. For example, one person makes $10,000 a year and another makes $100,000, but when they tithe, they both feel it the same. The sacrifice is identical because it is related to how much they make. However, when a person decides to go beyond the tithe and begins to give offerings, he has moved to another level in his giving. He is willingly presenting something to God—nobody is forcing him to. He just wants to do it, so he does. His offering is actually an act of worship given to the God he loves and adores.

Look at Psalm 96:6–9:

> Honor and majesty are before him: strength and beauty are in his sanctuary. ⁷Give unto the Lord, O ye kindreds of the people, give unto the Lord glory and strength. ⁸Give unto the Lord the glory due unto his name: bring an offering, and come into his courts. ⁹O worship the Lord in the beauty of holiness: fear before him, all the earth.

Notice how verse 8 speaks of giving God the glory, or praise, that He deserves, and verse 9 instructs us to worship Him. Right between those two verses, in the last part of verse 8, we are told to bring an offering to Him. So, you see, our offerings to God are sandwiched right in between our praise and worship of Him. It is an act of worship when we bring our offering to God!

An offering is not just some little old thing you throw around to this charity or that whenever the urge hits. That's all fine and good to give to worthy causes, but the offering I'm talking about is an intentional seed that you plant over and above the tithe. You do it because you want to, not because you have to. It is a reflection of your love and adoration of God.

In the Greek, the word *offering* actually means "to present," or "to make a present." In other words, it is a gift freely given. It's like on Christmas morning when you go to the tree and you have gifts there from those who love you. It's really not all that important as to what is in the box; you are blessed and happy because your loved ones gave you something that they selected just for you. But think how you would feel if you opened that box and inside the box was a note that said, "This present is from your wife (or anyone else). I really didn't want to give it to you, but I knew I had to fulfill my duty to you." If you're like me, you would just stop right there and forget the whole thing. You wouldn't even want the gift anymore because you would know it didn't come from a willing heart.

The same is true in our giving to God. The Bible says that God loves a cheerful giver (2 Cor. 9:7). That's why He never approves of anyone trying to manipulate people to give offerings. He's against those people or ministries that use gimmicks or guilt or underhanded methods to try to persuade people to give. Don't let anyone coerce you into giving more than you want to give through the leading of the Holy Spirit. If you do, your gift is not acceptable to the Lord; it's like the Christmas present given unwillingly. So bring your offering to God, willingly and with a cheerful heart, and as a gracious, loving Father, He will be delighted with it.

Offerings are a form of priestly worship. In the Old Testament, the priests' lives were totally dedicated to God. Their whole lives consisted of bringing offerings before the

Lord. Every day they brought to the Lord the sin offering or the peace offering or the thank offering. You can read about it all through the book of Leviticus. This was their job: to bring before the Lord offerings.

In the same way, the New Testament says that we are a "holy priesthood" called to "offer up spiritual sacrifices" (1 Pet. 2:5). Verse 9 continues by telling us that we are a "chosen generation, a royal priesthood" and are meant to "show forth the praises of him who hath called [us] out of darkness into his marvelous light." That's our job as New Testament priests: to give offerings to our God and to praise the one who has saved us and drawn us into His glorious light.

If you are in God's family, then you are part of that royal priesthood; therefore, everything in your life is holy, or sanctified. That means your job is holy, in the sense that because you are there and you are a royal priest, God will bless that place as you offer it to Him. Furthermore, your talents are holy. If God's given you the ability to sing or write or to do something else in an extraordinary fashion, don't just discount that talent and throw it on the trash heap. Consider that gift as holy and from the Lord. Offer it to Him for His use in His kingdom. Your ministry, your family, and whatever you are involved in are all holy because you are a royal priest.

The same is true concerning your offerings to the Lord. They are holy, and when you freely present them to the Lord, He is going to reward you openly. That's what the Word of God says. Look in Matthew 6. In this chapter of the Scriptures, Jesus is talking about almsgiving, prayer, and fasting. Each time, He admonishes His listeners to do their giving, praying, and fasting as a private act of worship to God, but then each time He also says how the Father will reward openly those who do so. In verses 4, 7, and 18, He repeats the phrase "Thy Father . . . shall reward thee openly."

Some people think the only reward or answer to their prayers they will ever get will be one day in the "sweet by and by" after they walk through the pearly gates. What they fail to realize, however, is that in heaven they will be living in perfection. They won't have to be praying for anything because they'll have everything. The need for prayer is during our time here on earth, and when we do pray, we are to make it an act of devotion to God, not a show for man. When we pray in this way, He is going to reward us openly.

It's the same for giving alms, an offering to the poor. Don't brag to everyone how much you help everybody else, and don't give because you want others to think highly of you. Give privately from your heart, and again God will reward you openly. That's what He did for Cornelius, the Gentile centurion in Acts 10. The Word of God says that Cornelius was a devout man who feared God, gave to the poor, and prayed regularly. These were his acts of worship to the God of Israel, and look how Cornelius was rewarded! You probably remember the story. In a vision, Peter was instructed to go to Joppa and minister salvation to Cornelius and his household. He obeyed God, and salvation came to the Gentiles as a result.

In Luke 11 Jesus had quite a bit to say to the Pharisees about giving and doing for God with right motives. After calling them fools in verse 40, He proceeded to say in verse 41, "But rather give alms of such things as ye have." You really can't give an offering out of something you don't have. It's just not there to be given. That's why you need to ask God to give you increased income. It's not so that you can have more cars, a bigger house, and more possessions. If that's the only reason you're believing for God to increase you, you're missing the point altogether. The better motive for asking for increased income is that you might be a channel of blessing to those in need around you.

Verse 42 of Luke 11 is a very interesting verse. Jesus commented on how the Pharisees meticulously tithed on every little seed that they had but neglected practicing justice and the love of God. The Pharisees never missed a beat in any aspect of tithing. They understood it and practiced it to the tiniest degree, and Jesus even said in verse 42 "these ought ye to have done," but tithing did not win them God's approval. They left undone the higher level of the law: giving to the poor and showing God's love and mercy.

Tithing, as even Jesus said, ought to be done, but you've got to understand that giving your offerings to the poor and others in need is a step above tithing. Think of it this way: Tithing opens the windows of heaven, but offerings bring the showers of blessing through those windows. God knows you are devout and disciplined when you tithe, but when you begin to give offerings, He knows that you have moved into the delight of giving to others. Then the blessings of God begin to pour into your life in abundance as you reap what you have sowed from a pure heart.

Luke 12:31 says it another way: "But rather seek ye the kingdom of God; and all these things shall be added unto you." What things are going to be added to you as you put

God first in your life? All things! That means utility bills, car payments, and mortgage notes. It means money for food, clothing, and education. When you tithe and give offerings above the tithe, you're placing your financial security on the shoulders of a God who wants to bless you. You don't have to beg Him or try to persuade Him to bless you. It is His "good pleasure to give you the kingdom" (Luke 12:32).

Go on to verse 33: "Sell that ye have, and give alms; provide yourselves bags which wax not old, a treasure in the heavens that faileth not, where no thief approacheth, neither moth corrupteth." Wouldn't it be great if one day you just decided to take all the junk you've been accumulating in your attic, put it out on the front lawn, and let it go to the highest bidder? You could let go of that old, rusty lawn mower and those clothes that you're never going to fit into again and just sell them. You could say, "Lord, whatever comes out of this, I'm going to give to world missions. I'm going to use it to extend Your kingdom somewhere in this world." Wouldn't that be glorious? When you do that, you are storing up eternal treasure in heaven!

Offerings as Seed

Luke 5 shows us another principle about our offerings. I talked about this story in the last chapter, but now I want to show you something else from it. Verse 1 describes Jesus on the seashore, with great hordes of people pressing upon Him. They might have been literally backing Him up to the very edge of the water. Thousands of people were present, I'm sure.

Down the beach a distance away were two guys washing their nets, their boats alongside them. They didn't seem to be particularly interested in Jesus; they were just there pursuing their livelihood. Can you imagine Jesus walking down the beach and coming up to Peter, saying, "I wonder if I could use your boat for a while?" Think about it. That's a pretty big request because Peter's boat was the way he made his living. It provided his source for income. Peter could have said, "Sir, I'm sorry, but I've got to leave, and, I don't really want anybody out in my boat while I'm gone." But instead he said, "My boat is your boat, Jesus. I give it to you. Take it and use it however you want." That was the greatest decision of his life!

The Lord of Glory, who created all the fish in the sea, all the oceans, mountains, and streams, all the creatures of the earth, and all mankind, asked Peter for the use of his boat. Peter didn't have any fish to offer the Lord, for he had caught nothing from the previous evening's outing, but he did have one valuable resource—his boat. That boat represented not only his talents and livelihood, but it also represented his need. He'd fished all night and caught nothing. In essence, therefore, what Peter did was take his need and plant it into the kingdom of God. He took that which his own energies had been unable to accomplish and said, "Lord, I sow that into Your work."

This was the crucial point of Peter's decision. The moment the King of Kings sat down in Peter's boat, it changed from a "natural" boat to a "supernatural" one. He pushed that boat from land a little bit, and He taught the people. When He finished speaking and everyone had left,

He turned to Peter (who obviously had gotten into the boat with Him) and said, "Launch out into the deep, and let down your nets for a draught" (v. 4).

Peter really didn't think it was any use to fish again when they had caught nothing all the night before, but he said, "At thy word I will let down the net." Because of his obedience, the Lord was able to give him "a great multitude of fishes" (v. 6). It doesn't say that He gave Peter a couple of minnows and a crab, but it says the Lord gave him a whole lot of fish!

The King knew right where the school was running, and He stopped the boat at just the right spot and said, "Right here; here's the spot, men. Just drop your net." When they dropped the net, it began to sag from the weight of all those fish. I can just hear Peter and the others moaning and groaning as they tried to hold on to that net and pull it aboard. Don't you know they were excited!

James and John were there with Peter, and I'll bet they were all shouting and tugging with all their might on that net. But God's abundance and blessing was so great that they couldn't pull it aboard. They needed help, so they started shouting to their partners in another boat to come and assist them. The overflowing provision of fish was so great that both boats were filled to sinking. Think about fish piled up so high in both boats that the edges of the boats sank right down to the edge of the water. That's abundance! That's increase! That's the very windows of heaven opened and pouring down a blessing too great to be contained!

When you freely give an offering to God and plant a seed from your need, the Lord responds delightedly. He says, like He did to Peter, "Now push out a little further and let your nets down into the deep." Oh, what a blessing to know that God is on your side! He longs to jump into the boat with you, take you out to the deepest waters, and fill you to overflowing with His abundance.

When you plant a seed out of your need, it's like Jesus is saying, "Thank you, I'll use that in the service of the kingdom of God. I'm going to receive that seed, bring it out to the deep waters, and fill it with so much power that your boat will nearly sink." I don't know about you, but I could use a boat-sinking harvest—in my finances, my family, my ministry, and every area of my life!

That's one of the most basic parts to seeing God increase you more and more. Find a "boat," something that may not seem like much to anyone else, but to you represents sowing from your need into the kingdom of God. There were probably better boats than Peter's, but his was the one the Lord used and blessed because of its availability.

Remember the little boy in the Scriptures with the five loaves and two fishes? That's not really much of a lunch. Probably lots of people had more and better food they could have offered. It was this child, however, who willingly gave what he had for the Master's use. That little boy said, "Here, Jesus. You can have my lunch. It's not a lot, but it's Yours." He placed his offering in the hands of the Lord, and Jesus took that small thing and multiplied it many, many times over, feeding five thousand men, along with their wives and children. In fact, the multiplication was so great that there were twelve baskets left over!

The principle of sowing from your need is demonstrated

time after time in the Bible. In the Old Testament, a widow gave Elijah the little bit of flour and oil she was saving for her son and herself. Because she gave from her desperate need, God returned it to her many times over, sustaining her through three and a half more years of famine (1 Kings 17:8–16). If she would have refused to give when it was asked of her, she and her son would probably have enjoyed their last meager meal together and then died when the oil and flour ran out. Her obedience, however, resulted in day-after-day provision. Every morning she got up, mixed her oil and flour, and poured out the pancakes for breakfast. Every day there was enough. It defied all logical explanation, but somehow her oil and flour lasted through all the time of famine.

Offerings as Investment

Your seed is an investment, really. Peter, the little boy with the loaves and fishes, and the widow all found that out. And people today, in my church and yours, are finding that out, too. I was so blessed when a woman in our church came up to me and shared her story of sowing from her need. This woman was a single parent with not many financial resources. In fact, she had been doing without central heat in her home for a couple of years because she couldn't afford it. She came to church one morning and heard a representative from the Gideons speak about placing Bibles all around the world. She wanted to sow a seed into that ministry, but all she had was $5. She decided to give what she had, and as she cheerfully and willingly placed her

The Laws of Increase

offering in the bucket, she prayed, "Lord, I am believing you for central heat in my home."

She gave her offering on Sunday, and on Tuesday her boss approached her and said he wanted to repair her heating system. He sent a repair crew, spent the $1200 needed to get the system working, and the woman had the heat she had prayed for! That was a quick return on her investment, to be sure.

I'm not talking about using God like He is some type of celestial slot machine. No, that is not right at all. He cannot be dictated to: "God, I'll do this; then you do that"—and then "cha-ching," you hit the jackpot. It never works that way. I'm talking about being a royal priest, knowing that everything you have belongs to God and wanting to invest your resources—whatever they are—into His kingdom. God, in turn, is no man's debtor, and He will repay in His own time and way. You can bank on that fact.

Many outstanding business leaders that love the Lord have made a commitment to honor the Lord in their businesses and to give back to the community or those less fortunate from the bounty of their increase. As they have prospered, they have sowed into the kingdom of God, and it seems God just keeps giving back to them more and more. I think about Truett Cathy, the founder of the Chick-fil-A restaurant chain. From its humble beginnings in 1946, the restaurant has declared a solid, godly basis for its existence. In their own words, they state that they exist "to glorify God by being a faithful steward of all that is entrusted to us and to have a positive influence on all who come in contact with Chick-fil-A" (<http://www.chickfila.com/Company.asp> n.d.,

December 4, 2003). To achieve their missions statement, they close all their restaurants on Sundays, provide millions of dollars in scholarship programs, and invest heavily in foster homes and community service projects.

Chick-fil-A is just one of many companies, small businesses, and individuals who have willingly sowed seed into the kingdom of God and been blessed beyond their wildest expectations. These people know that any talent or ability they possess is not really theirs. They realize that giving is not so much about letting go of something as it is about taking the resources that God has given and investing them in something that will multiply in the lives of others. They perpetuate an ongoing cycle of investing and reinvesting in the kingdom of God and the lives of others. That is the real principle of the offering: investing the resources that God gives into strategic areas that multiply in the lives of others.

Offerings to Reap Souls

Some people have very narrow vision concerning their giving. All they see and think about is how God is going to increase their finances and bless them materially. It's true that God is concerned about those things, but I encourage you to stretch your faith and vision for increase to include so much more than mere financial provision. As you plant your seed in the kingdom of God, look for the increase in a harvest of souls to your account. That is true riches, far beyond the value of any earthly possessions.

Let's look again at our story in Luke 5. As I mentioned

earlier, Jesus got into Peter's boat and sat down. All indications from that chapter seem to point to the fact that Peter did not show some great interest in Jesus (he was busy cleaning his nets), but Jesus took a great interest in him. Jesus reached out to him and took the initiative in the relationship.

Peter was washing his net that he used in his business. His time was spent pursuing those things that were of interest to him. Jesus didn't send a messenger to Peter to say, "Peter, you are missing the greatest revival service in history." Neither did Jesus go to Peter and say, "Now, Peter, you need to repent. Do you know the 'Four Spiritual Laws'? Have you heard the 'Roman Road' plan of salvation?" He didn't do any of that. He simply sat down in Peter's boat.

There's a lesson to be learned here. You will not increase as a soul-winner just by learning more facts about winning souls. The increase will not come by some new method or strategy you or your cell group thinks up. The increase comes when you offer your time and love and get into somebody's boat. It's much more powerful and effective when you demonstrate the Gospel to someone through the love and interest you show than when you just preach the Gospel in words.

You've got to enter the world of the lost. Sometimes we act like we think lost people just can't wait to come to our church. We think they are sitting around, so interested in us and what we are doing. More times than not, however, that is not the case! Most of them would rather sleep late, play golf, or watch TV on a Sunday morning. They're not interested in our church, cell groups, or special music. They are

The Laws of Increase

interested primarily in themselves and their interests.

They don't want to listen to us talk about our church—how wonderful it is, how nice the new parking lot is, how beautiful the new building is going to be. They want to talk about themselves! So when you minister to the lost, stop talking about yourself and let them talk about what interests them. You should know their name, and address them by name as you speak. Then you need to find out what they are interested in by asking questions that get them talking. Find something you can build a common base on and start there. Finally, begin spending time with them, getting to know them as individuals, not just as faceless souls to be added to your spiritual belt of accomplishments. It's not a five- or ten-minute proposition to win a soul—it's a commitment to building a relationship with a very real person.

Of course, I'm not talking about becoming all things to everyone to the extent that you have no more boundaries of any kind. You're not going to hang out in the bars and drink with the drunkards so that you can "relate" to them. You're not going to engage in sin or inappropriate behavior of any kind under the pretext of reaching out to others. The devil may try to lead you down that path, but you've got to know that's not God's way. God's way has you reaching out to others, motivated by love and compassion. You enter their world in a sincere way, trying to understand what makes them tick, what they are struggling with, and what they need.

That's exactly what Jesus did. When He got into Peter's boat, He didn't say, "Isn't it wonderful how all these people came to hear Me preach? Do you want Me to summarize My message for you?" He turned to Peter and said, "Let down your net. I'm going to give you some fish!" He recognized Peter's need and met him there. When He did that, notice what happened to Peter. Verse 8 of Luke 5 records his response: "Depart from me; for I am a sinful man, O Lord." The goodness of God led him to repentance, and as you show love and compassion to others and meet their needs, their hearts will soften, like Peter's did, and they'll want to know this Savior that you represent.

People who love the Lord find very creative ways to minister to the lost around them. Nairobi Lighthouse Church in Nairobi, Kenya, decided to start reaching out to their neighborhoods by meeting the needs of the community. Cell groups went out and walked around the area, trying to determine what the neighborhood needed. If they saw a clogged sewer, they decided to clean it. On their cell meeting night, they would gather equipment, go to the neighborhood, and begin doing the dirty work of unclogging the sewer. Inevitably people would gather around, wanting to know what they were doing. The Christians would simply tell them who they were and where they were from and that they wanted to bless the community. In one housing estate where they did this, the practical work done by the cell members led to their being allowed to have a cell meeting in the community the following week, with thirty-three people getting saved!

Those Kenyans had found a way to reach the lost. They simply looked around and found a need that they could meet. They demonstrated the love of Christ in a practical way, and God returned that investment of time and energy to them in the form of a harvest of souls. That's the kind of increase I want! I'm going to invest my time and talents in the lives of others. I'm going to make an investment in the kingdom of God. I'm going to release my faith and present my offering to God with a willing heart of love. And God is going to increase me more and more!

CHAPTER 3

Waiting for Increase

No one likes to wait! Ours is an impatient society, characterized by drive-through convenience, microwave quickness, and instant gratification. Most of us expect to have what we want when we want it, and heaven help the one who gets in our way! We get upset when we miss the green light and can't stand to wait in line at the bank. We fume when the doctor keeps us waiting and complain when the preacher talks too long. It seems that every day of our lives we're forced to wait for something, and we don't like it.

Waiting, however, is an inescapable part of life, and patience, a much needed virtue. No matter how restless you are, it still takes nine months for a baby to be ready to be born, twelve years to graduate from high school, and 365 days for Christmas to come again. That's just the way it is, and no amount of ranting and raving on your part is going to change it.

Patience for the Harvest

In the spiritual realm, waiting is an integral part of the process of seeing God's increase come into your life. It's the third aspect in the sower's heart. First was the *sacrifice* of increase; then came the *offering* of increase. In this chapter, we're ready to look at *waiting* for increase. In the process of sowing and reaping, you've got to understand this ingredient called "waiting." Without it, you will never see increase in your finances, character, or souls won to Christ, but with it, you will discover one of the most basic ingredients to having God increase you more and more. James 5:7–11 has quite a bit to say about this important aspect of increase:

> Be patient therefore, brethren, unto the coming of the Lord. Behold, the husbandman waiteth for the precious fruit of the earth, and hath long patience for it, until he receive the early and latter rain. [8]Be ye also patient; stablish your hearts: for the coming of the Lord draweth nigh. [9]Grudge not one against another, brethren, lest ye be condemned: behold, the judge standeth before the door. [10]Take, my brethren, the prophets, who have spoken in the name of the Lord, for an example of suffering affliction, and of patience. [11]Behold, we count them happy which endure. Ye have heard of the patience of Job, and have seen the end of the Lord; that the Lord is very pitiful, and of tender mercy.

When you start sowing seed for an increase in some area of your life, you are going to have to exercise patience. To

The Laws of Increase

some of you, patience is a dirty word. You don't want to be told that God expects you to wait. But look how our passage from James starts: "Be patient." Then it goes on to talk about a farmer who plants his seed and then waits patiently for the harvest. After planting our seed, most of us are tempted to go out the next day and dig it up to see if it's working yet. That would never work in the natural world, and it won't work in the spiritual world, either.

There is a natural progression to growth: "first the blade, then the ear, after that the full corn in the ear" (Mark 4:28). The farmer has no choice but to wait patiently for the crop to grow. While he is waiting, he goes about his business—eating and sleeping and carrying on with the thousands of details of everyday life. He doesn't fret and fume over the seed he planted because he knows that "the earth bringeth forth fruit of herself" (Mark 4:28). It is an irrefutable principle, and he knows that within himself he has no power to make even the tiniest seed sprout.

Just as you can't bypass the natural laws of sowing and reaping, you can't get around the spiritual laws of increase. When you plant spiritual seed, you need to have the same assurance the farmer has when he plants. You've got to let God's natural progression take place and not be constantly worrying about whether the seed you planted is growing yet.

James talks about the "early rain" and the "latter rain" in regards to the harvest. In the Middle East, farmers are dependent on an early rain to make their fields ready for planting and a latter rain six to eight months later right before harvest time. Between the early and latter rains, they have to wait. It's a part of the process, and they can't get around it.

It's the same way for you when you sow a spiritual seed. The fact that you sow financial seed or show an act of love to someone or give one witness of the Gospel does not mean that you're going to see instant harvest. Like the farmer, you're going to have to learn to wait. The "rain" of God's Spirit is going to have to fall and do its part in bringing forth the harvest. Until the rain comes, you are powerless; you are totally dependent upon its work, and you simply have to wait for it.

Some plants, such as bamboo, grow very slowly for the first several years. Each spring, only a few new shoots come up, and to the untrained eye, it seems as though nothing much is happening. After three or four years, however, something remarkable occurs. In that year, the bamboo suddenly sends up many shoots, and the growth is quite phenomenal. Some species have even been known to grow as much as four feet in just one day! That tremendous growth seems to come all at once, but really, it has been years in the making. While waiting for the increase, the farmer doesn't go out into his field and pull up the bamboo to see if it is growing. He knows it is, even if he can't see much evidence of it. Throughout those first years of imperceptible growth, he patiently waits. He knows the year of harvest is coming!

Galatians 6:7 says, "Be not deceived; God is not mocked: for whatsoever a man soweth, that shall he also reap." Verse 9 then gives us the condition: "And let us not be weary in well doing: for in due season we shall reap, if we faint not." There is a due season to reap! If you've been praying for a particular person and trying to win him to the Lord, don't grow weary in the process. Continue spending time with him, taking an interest in what interests him and making a sincere effort to get involved in his life. In due season, you'll reap his soul for the kingdom of God.

Maybe you've been sowing financial seed and it feels like you are waiting and waiting and waiting for the expected harvest. Don't faint, brothers and sisters; don't even give it a second thought. Your "due season" could be just around the corner! Just say, "Thank you, Lord. My time is coming. I may not know when and I might not know how, but I'm not worried about it. I'm going to continue to sow into Your kingdom, and You *will* increase me more and more."

Lessons of Waiting

When you sow your seed, that's the easy part. When you look down the road and see the reaping that will come, that's the fun part. But in between those two points is that period of time called "waiting." Most of the time, you are going to have this span of time between when you sow and when you reap. I believe that God often requires a waiting time because He has certain things He wants to do in you during that season. While you are patiently waiting for your harvest, God is at work in your life, testing you to see if He can entrust you with a bountiful increase. Let's look at three areas of testing.

The testing of your heart

You will never be able to handle increase if the motives of your heart are not right. If you are just interested in "what's in it for me," you'll never be a good steward over any increase. God has to reveal to you the true state of your heart so that you can be a sower that is pleasing to Him.

Exodus 23:28–30 says, "And I will send hornets before thee, which shall drive out the Hivite, the Canaanite, and the Hittite, from before thee. I will not drive them out from before thee in one year; lest the land become desolate, and the beast of the field multiply against thee. By little and little I will drive them out from before thee, until thou be increased, and inherit the land." God told the Israelites that "little by little" He would increase them, until finally they would inherit the land He intended for them. He had valid reasons for what He did, too; He wasn't just trying to make them wait for the sake of waiting. He knew that He could not increase their possession of the land until He had worked increase in them.

That's the way He deals with us. We generally increase little by little because most of us couldn't handle sudden, overabundant increase. God has to test our hearts to see how we will handle the increase. He has to ask Himself, "If I increase them, what's it going to do to them? Is it going to destroy them? Will they claim credit for the increase? Are they really ready for increase?" For most of us, if God removed all our financial problems and made us billionaires overnight, it would be more than we could handle. Some of us, sad to say, would become so puffed up as to be useless to the kingdom of God.

So He works the increase in our lives a little bit at a time. Most of the time you can't even tell that you are increasing because it's such a gradual thing. But after a while, you notice that things are different. There's more left over at the end of the month, or your lost relatives start to respond to the Gospel. You didn't notice it while it was happening, but all of a sudden you realize how you've been blessed.

When God increases you gradually, He is testing you, watching what you do in whatever circumstance you are in. In the verses in Exodus, God spoke to His people as they left Egypt and told them how the increase would come. Forty years later as they were poised to move into the Promised Land, He reminded them of it again: "And the Lord thy God will put out those nations before thee by little and little: thou mayest not consume them at once, lest the beasts of the field increase upon thee" (Deut. 7:22). For forty years, God's people had been roaming in the wilderness. Even though their lack of faith and obedience had put them there, God had a work He was doing in them during that time. "And thou shalt remember all the way which the Lord thy God led thee these forty years in the wilderness, to humble thee, and to prove thee, to know what was in thine heart, whether thou wouldest keep his commandments, or no" (Deut. 8:22).

The time in the desert was necessary to humble them and to prove them before God. Now most of us don't want any part of that! We want God to lift us up, bless us, and exalt us, and He does want to do that. But we're probably going to have to go through some things before we reach that stage. As humans, we have a natural tendency to become proud, and God has to deal with that before He can bless us.

God wants to know what is in your heart, and He is going to test you so that your inner motives can be revealed. He wants to be sure that when He brings the increase that He's promised, it won't change you one bit. He wants to know that with blessing, you'll continue to walk with Him, obeying His commands. He's got to prove your heart.

In the wilderness, God fed His people with manna, keeping them dependent upon Him and His provision. They had to learn that He was their source of sustenance. For forty years they roamed through the desert, and God was watching. They had His promise of a rich, abundant land, but before that promise came to pass, they spent all those years humbly picking up manna, waiting for the time of the promise to be fulfilled. Nevertheless, God was still with them, taking care of them every step of the way. In verse 4 of Deuteronomy 8, we read how He even made sure their clothes didn't wear out and their feet did not swell (meaning their shoes didn't wear out). In the midst of the wilderness and the time of testing, God was there, supernaturally feeding and caring for His people.

When you are walking through your time of testing, never forget that God is with you. He can cause that old car of yours to continue working long past what you would expect. He'll see to it that you have food in your pantry. He'll stretch your dollar far beyond everyone else's. He will provide for you in every way, but He will also be watching you while you're in that waiting period. He wants to see what's in your heart.

The Laws of Increase

Look at verses 7–9 in Deuteronomy 8:

> For the Lord thy God bringeth thee into a good land, a land of brooks of water, of fountains and depths that spring out of valleys and hills; [8]A land of wheat, and barley, and vines, and fig trees, and pomegranates; a land of oil olive, and honey; [9]A land wherein thou shalt eat bread without scarceness, thou shalt not lack any thing in it; a land whose stones are iron, and out of whose hills thou mayest dig brass.

God's ultimate purpose is to bless you—after you've proved yourself faithful in the wilderness. He wants to give you a good land. He doesn't want you feeding in some little old poverty-stricken pasture. He wants to give you a land flowing with water, grain, and fruit—a land without scarceness. That's His desire for you. But He's got to be sure that you can handle the increase. Verses 10–14 prove that:

> When thou hast eaten and art full, then thou shalt bless the Lord thy God for the good land which he hath given thee. [11]Beware that thou forget not the Lord thy God, in not keeping his commandments, and his judgments, and his statutes, which I command thee this day: [12]Lest when thou hast eaten and art full, and hast built goodly houses, and dwelt therein; [13]And when thy herds and thy flocks multiply, and thy silver and thy gold is multiplied, and all that thou hast is multiplied; [14]Then thine heart be lifted up, and thou forget the Lord thy God. . . .

The Laws of Increase

There is always that danger that you will forget the Lord when He increases you, that you will say, "My power and the might of my hand have gained me this wealth" (v. 17). I've seen that happen. I've watched people sow into the kingdom of God, and then when they begin reaping a blessing, they start analyzing what's happened. They begin thinking, "I sure am smart to come up with that idea. I've really got it all together." Brothers and sisters, that's a dangerous place to be in. God is watching your heart, and He wants you to respond with gratitude and humility when a little increase comes so that He can entrust you with more increase.

It's sort of like a scuba diver. He can go down into the depths of the ocean, but when he comes back up, he's got to do it very slowly. He's got to allow the air pressure to gradually increase as he ascends. If he were to shoot up from the bottom to the top, he would kill himself because his body could not tolerate the rapid increase in pressure. In the same way, God can't increase you too fast. He increases you little by little because He cares about your heart. He wants you to remember that He is the one who gives you power to get wealth in order that His covenant may be established (v. 18).

Do you remember the covenant God made with Abraham? He told him that He would increase him (Gen. 15:5) and through him all the nations of the earth would be blessed (Gen. 18:18). God wants to bless the nations of the world through His people, and that means you! His plan is not to bless you just so you can have the most expensive, latest model car sitting behind your million-dollar mansion. He wants to bless you so that through you His covenant can be extended throughout all the earth.

If I asked you, "Wouldn't you love to have millions to give to world missions?" most of you would say, "Oh, yes, Brother Larry, I would love to have millions to give to the work of the Lord." Stop for a minute and think about it. Would you really give it away if you had it, or would you squander it on material things that have no eternal value?

God is in covenant with you, and He wants to use you to spread His kingdom around the world. Start believing God for seed to sow. Ask Him specifically for it, and when it comes, give it away. Don't hoard it for yourself and eat the seed that God provides. Examine your heart—that's the important thing. As God increases you, are you going to blow up like a bullfrog, full of pride and smugness? Or, are you going to say, "Look what the Lord has done! He's given me seed to establish His covenant in Afghanistan and Turkey and China. I can win thousands of souls with this money." If that's the attitude of your heart, then God can entrust you with a bountiful, overflowing harvest.

The testing of your faithfulness

In addition to testing your heart, God is going to test your faithfulness. Jesus said in Luke 16:10 that if you are faithful in little things, you will be faithful in larger things. During the time while you're waiting for your seed to grow, God is testing your faithfulness. He's watching to see if you just keep giving faithfully whatever amount you have to sow. He wants to know that you will be faithful with a small amount before He can give you a larger amount.

I know of no better example in the Bible of faithfulness and its rewards than the life of Jacob. He went through twenty years of testing and wilderness experiences before he really began to prosper, but he remained faithful to God. You probably remember his story. Born the younger of a set of twins, Jacob first wrangled the birthright from his older brother, Esau, and then deceived his father, Isaac, into giving him the blessing of the firstborn. Because of his actions, he was forced to flee his home and set out for his Uncle Laban's house in Paddan Aram.

The very first night of his journey, he had a dream from God, in which he saw angels ascending a ladder into heaven. There he was—all alone in the wilderness—running for his life and lying with his head on a rock for a pillow. When you're sleeping out in an open field and you have to pull up a rock to use as your pillow, you're facing a trial—big time! You're experiencing what we call "looking up to see bottom."

That's where Jacob was. But he had a dream in which God told him He would bless him and increase him. When Jacob awoke he took his "pillow" and turned it into a "pillar," vowing, "If God will be with me, and will keep me in this way that I go, and will give me bread to eat, and raiment to put on . . . of all that thou shalt give me I will surely give the tenth unto thee" (Gen. 28:21, 22). Here was Jacob, a man who lived before the Law was given, vowing to give God a tenth, or a tithe, of whatever God would give him. The tithe had already been established by his grandfather, Abraham, and now Jacob was embracing this principle, too. And, as we'll see a little later, he fulfilled his promise to God.

Many people make promises to God, but not everyone

The Laws of Increase

keeps them. It's easy to say when you don't have any money in your pocket, "Lord, I'll tithe. Whatever You give me, I'll give a tenth back to You." The test of your commitment and faithfulness comes when God starts answering your prayer and you have money to give. What do you do then?

I heard a story about a man who went to church, asking for prayer to get a job. He said, "Pastor, pray for me. I need a job. If the Lord will bless me, I'll tithe." The pastor prayed for him, and the man got a job and began tithing. He continued to prosper financially until after a couple of years he realized that he was making so much money that he was now tithing $50,000 a year!

He went back to the pastor and said, "Pastor, I don't think I'm going to be able to tithe anymore. I'm giving so much to the church now, and since my tithe has increased to $50,000 a year, I don't know if I can afford it anymore."

The pastor said, "That's fine; kneel down and let me pray for God to decrease you to your former level when you could afford to tithe." Needless to say, the man quickly had a change of heart.

After Jacob made his vow to God, he proceeded on his way until he arrived at Laban's house. Jacob had been a deceiver all his life, but in Laban he met someone who was even more of a trickster than he. Laban was as slippery as a snake, a little beady-eyed guy who was out to get what he could. Jacob served Laban for seven years for the privilege of marrying his daughter Rachel. On the wedding day, however, Laban slipped in Leah in place of Rachel. Now Jacob had to work seven more years to earn the right to marry the girl he was supposed to get in the first place.

The Laws of Increase

Jacob continued to work with Laban, and after a number of years, he decided to ask for a portion of the flocks. Notice what Jacob said in verse 29 of Genesis 30: "For it was little which thou hadst before I came, and it is now increased unto a multitude." Acknowledging that fact, Laban then asked Jacob what he wanted, and Jacob asked for all the speckled and spotted sheep and goats. Laban readily agreed, but then he removed all the speckled and spotted animals before Jacob could take possession of them.

Jacob, however, kept tending Laban's flocks. He took some small branches from the trees, peeled them to reveal white streaks, and set them in front of the watering troughs. The sheep would look at those rods, and when it was breeding season, they mated before them, producing streaked and spotted offspring. He used the rods only before the stronger sheep, thereby increasing the strength as well as the number in his flock. As a result, verse 43 tells us that Jacob "increased exceedingly." He didn't just increase, but he increased exceedingly, regardless of the fact that Laban had tried to keep him from prospering.

When God decides to increase you, no man can stop His mighty hand! It didn't matter what Laban did—Jacob prospered anyway. When Laban saw Jacob prospering, he couldn't stand it, so he said that he wanted the speckled sheep. Jacob gave them to him, and then the other sheep began increasing. Whatever Jacob touched just seemed to automatically increase. Jacob knew that God was his source, and it didn't matter what any man tried to do. To his wives, he made this statement concerning their father, Laban: "And ye know that with all my power I have served your father. And your father hath deceived me, and changed my wages ten times; but God suffered him not to hurt me" (Gen. 31:6).

I don't care if you work for an ornery, stingy boss. He might be ugly to you and tell you you're never going to get a raise. He might delight in making life miserable for you, but don't pay any attention to him. Don't look to him as your source—look to God alone. When you tithe and give offerings, you're not under your employer's economic rules; you're under the economy of the kingdom of heaven! God knows what's going on, and He will move heaven and earth on your behalf. He told Jacob that He had seen exactly what Laban had done (v. 12), and He knows what's going on in your life, too.

When Jacob finally returned to his father's land, he had increased so much that he could say, "With my staff I passed over this Jordan; and now I am become two bands" (Gen. 32:10). The "pauper" had become a "prince," and Jacob had more wealth and provision than he would ever need. Because he was faithful in little, God blessed him with much. He is waiting to do the same for you.

Another good example of someone who was faithful even in the midst of terrible circumstances was Joseph, the son of Jacob and Rachel. Joseph, it seemed, got the raw end of every deal that came his way. His own brothers sold him into slavery, and according to some sources, he remained a slave for more than thirteen years. Even as a slave in Potiphar's house, however, he prospered, as Genesis 39:2–3 says: "And the Lord was with Joseph, and he was a prosperous man; and he was in the house of his master the Egyptian.

The Laws of Increase

And his master saw that the Lord was with him, and that the Lord made all that he did to prosper in his hand."

One day Potiphar's wife falsely accused Joseph, and he was thrown into prison. Even there, again, God blessed him: "But the Lord was with Joseph, and showed him mercy, and gave him favor in the sight of the keeper of the prison. . . . The keeper of the prison looked not to any thing that was under his hand; because the Lord was with him, and that which he did, the Lord made it to prosper" (Gen. 39:21, 23). I'm telling you, if you'll just be faithful, it doesn't matter where you are or what you're doing. It really is irrelevant what kind of wilderness experience you're walking through when you realize that God can increase you anyway. Just be faithful—faithful in tithing, faithful in offerings, faithful in showing Christlike behavior, faithful in prayer, faithful in all aspects of life. Keep sowing the seed, and one day, like it happened for Joseph, you'll be loosed from your "prison."

When Joseph was about thirty years old, Pharaoh had a dream that he couldn't understand. God gave the interpretation to none other than Joseph—the young man who had come to Egypt as a slave and was now languishing in prison. Within a matter of minutes, Joseph went from the "outhouse" to the "White House," so to speak. He was released from the pit and went to the palace, right to Pharaoh's side. He interpreted the dream, and as a result, great honor and blessings were bestowed upon him.

God so wants to bless you, but before He can, He must test your faithfulness to Him. Do you waver in the time of trial? Do you question God when you don't understand what is going on? Do you renege on your word to Him when the going gets rough? If you do any of these things, you're not being faithful, and you are, in effect, delaying the increase that God wants to bring into your life.

On the other hand, if you set your face like a flint to serve God, if you keep your promises to Him, if you keep putting one foot in front of the other even when you can't see the path before you—if you keep doing all these things, the increase will come. It's inevitable because we serve a God of infinite blessing and increase.

The testing of your patience

First, God tests your heart; next, He tests your faithfulness; and finally, He tests your patience. Most of us are sorely lacking in this virtue, but it is so necessary before increase can come.

I remember a story my dad told me about a cousin of his who was driving in New Orleans when his car engine died at a red light. I'm sure New Orleans' drivers are no more impatient than drivers anywhere else, but when the man behind my dad's cousin realized that he was being delayed, he did what people everywhere do—he started blowing his horn. First it was just a couple of beeps, but as the seconds ticked by and Dad's cousin still couldn't start the car, the man behind him decided to make his point more forcefully. He just laid on that horn—one, long continuous beeeeeeeeeep! Dad's cousin calmly got out of his car, taking the key with him, walked back to where the other guy was, and said, "Here's the key. You go start my car, and I'll stay back here and help you along by blowing the horn."

A lot of us are like that. We think if we lay on the horn long enough and blow it loud enough, we can speed God along. Needless to say, it doesn't work that way. God requires patience from us, and until we learn that lesson, we will be forever trying to make something happen before its time.

Psalm 112:5 NIV says that "good will come to him who is generous and lends freely." It will come, but you have to be persuaded of that fact, knowing that if you sow, you will grow. Verse 6 says, "Surely he shall not be moved forever: the righteous shall be in everlasting remembrance." Nothing can move the person who knows God's increase is coming. Verses 7–8 reveal why: "He shall not be afraid of evil tidings: his heart is fixed, trusting in the Lord. His heart is established, he shall not be afraid, until he see his desire upon his enemies." The one who has learned the lesson of patience is not afraid when circumstances look bad. His heart is "fixed" on God, meaning he is trusting totally in God and is therefore unafraid. His heart is "established," waiting patiently for God to act.

You cannot get in a hurry. You've got to sit down and rest in the promises of God and say, "Lord, I've sowed my seed and I know it's growing." When someone comes along and says, "My, you have less and less every time I see you," you just say, "No, by faith, I've sowed my seed. I don't know where the increase is going to come from, but I know it's coming. My heart is fixed on my God."

Verse 9 of Psalm 112 continues, "He hath dispersed, he hath given to the poor; his righteousness endureth forever; his horn shall be exalted with honor." You've got to be

The Laws of Increase

convinced that if you tithe and give offerings to missions and to the poor, your horn will be exalted, your needs will be met, and your patience will be rewarded.

Look finally at verse 10 of this psalm: "The wicked shall see it, and be grieved; he shall gnash with his teeth, and melt away: the desire of the wicked shall perish." Can't you just see it! One day the devil's going to look at you, and you're going to be so blessed that he can't stand it! He's going to be gnashing with his teeth and will just have to melt away from you. Oh, hallelujah, what a glorious word! Hang in there, brothers and sisters, even if you're in the bottom of the ninth inning and the score is 10-0. Don't ever give up, because at your lowest moment, Jesus steps up to bat and hits the ball over the fence!

The New Testament echoes the same thought of patient waiting for the increase. In fact, in 2 Corinthians 9:9, verse 9 of Psalm 112 is quoted. Paul reminds us of the blessing awaiting those who have dispersed their gifts and sowed willingly into the kingdom of God. If you back up to verse 8 in 2 Corinthians 9, you see a wonderful statement: "God is able to make all grace abound toward you; that ye, always having all sufficiency in all things, may abound to every good work."

God is able! I don't care how long you've been waiting. If you've sowed seed, scattered abroad, cared for the poor ahead of your own needs, and put God's kingdom purposes first, then He is able to shower you with grace so that you will have enough for yourself and for others. That means you will be self-sufficient, not requiring aid and support from others. If you will start today to have that sower's heart, if you will give the sacrifice of your tithe and then heartfelt offerings, if you will be patient and wait for the increase, it will surely come!

CHAPTER 4

Expecting the Increase

What a joy to be a sower in the kingdom of God! It's a joy to give the *sacrifice* of the tithe. It's a wonderful privilege to be able to give *offerings* above the tithe. And *waiting* on God as He works increase in our lives, though not always easy, is vital if we are to develop a sower's heart. After studying sacrifice, offering, and waiting—the first three laws of increase—we're ready to learn about the "E" in SOWER. That letter in our acronym stands for the fourth principle of increase, that is, *expecting* your increase.

If you learn how to sacrifice, how to give offerings, and how to wait for God, but you don't learn how to expect your increase, you'll be stymied right at this point as you try to become a sower in God's work. That, unfortunately, is what happens to many people. They tithe faithfully and even give missions offerings. Day in and day out, year after year, they continue giving faithfully to the kingdom of God. But somewhere along the way, they lose their expectancy of ever seeing an increase in their lives. Their giving has become just a ritual—something they do—but they fail to make the connection between possessing increase and the expectancy that actually brings it to pass.

Psalm 62:5 tells us about expectancy: "My soul, wait thou only upon God; for my expectation is from him." God alone is the one to look to for the increase. Maybe you've been looking to your employer to do something for you, or maybe you've been expecting your spouse to meet all your emotional needs. Stop expecting anybody to do anything for you, and start expecting God to do everything for you! Look only to Him; "wait thou only upon God."

Some people lie awake upon their beds at night, worrying about their finances and trying to figure out how they're going to have enough. Somebody once said, "Two plus two equals four in the natural, but two plus two can equal a thousand when God is in the equation." That's the problem for some of you: You've left God completely out of the equation. If that's the case, two plus two will always equal four for you.

When you look to God as your source, however, you can't help but start expecting something to happen. The word *expect* is derived from the Latin word *exspectare* and means "to look forward to" and "to look at." So when you're expecting God to move and bring the increase into your life, you're looking for it. It's like you're eagerly leaning forward, straining to see it on the horizon. In other words, expectancy in God is really faith in Him.

When the lame man at the Gate Beautiful in Acts 3:5 saw Peter and John, he expected to receive something from them. Because of that expectant faith, Peter and John were

The Laws of Increase

able to give him something of far greater value than silver or gold. They gave him the gift of healing that he so desperately needed (vv. 6–8).

I like one definition I heard for expectancy: Expectancy is looking for a blessing to arrive at any moment while patiently waiting should it take forever! That's hard for most of us. Expectation, for many of us, is the missing ingredient in our faith life. We get so tired of the waiting, that soon we lose our expectancy. If in the time of waiting we can say like David, "My expectation is from Him," then we'll see the increase.

I don't know why God has that time between "amen" and "there it is," but He does. When you're waiting for increase, just keep your eyes on the Lord and look for the breakthrough as though it could happen at any moment. Don't give in to discouragement, saying, "I don't think my increase is ever coming." It won't if you keep believing and saying that. But if you continue sowing your seed, waiting patiently for your harvest and looking expectantly for it, you'll not be disappointed. The increase will surely come.

What are you expecting from God? Ask yourself that question, and you'll know what you're looking for. If you don't expect anything, you won't recognize it when it comes, and if you are expecting a harvest, you're going to be getting everything ready to contain it. Your actions reveal your expectations.

A pastor friend of mine told me a funny story about expectation. When he got saved, he was delivered from a life of drugs and drug dealing in New Orleans. God called him to preach and he obeyed, but he was as rough as a corncob after spending so much time on the street. He wasn't quite knowledgeable of all the proper "preacher ways" he needed to learn. When he performed his first wedding, the bride and groom had selected a song they wanted played on a cassette right after they were pronounced husband and wife, but before they kissed. When the moment came in the ceremony, my friend pronounced them husband and wife, but the cassette failed to play. There was some type of mechanical failure, so the pastor went ahead and told them to kiss. The bride, however, was waiting for the song and looked at the pastor and said, "Is that all?" Not knowing what to say, the rough young pastor blurted out, "Well, what do you expect for $25!" Of course, he has now learned a little more, but, nevertheless, the story illustrates a point. If you have a "$25 expectancy" from God, that's what you're going to get, but if you have a "$1,000 expectancy," that's what you're going to get. It all depends on what you're looking for.

Expect to receive vision!

When you are expecting increase, there are three main things you should be expecting, the first of which is vision. This is probably the most important aspect in receiving your increase. Until God gives you the vision of your increase, you have no faith to receive it, but once you see the vision, you know that you know that you know that it's coming! Remember how God gave Abraham a vision for descendants too numerous to count? He took Abraham outside and told him to count the stars, if indeed he could. That's how many offspring God would give him (Gen. 15:5). He gave

Abraham a vision, and then Abraham believed God (v. 6).

Expectation comes first from vision. I like the way Brother Myles Munroe explains it. He says that God knows the end from the beginning in any situation of life; thus, God first goes to the end of a thing and finishes it. Then He backs up to the beginning and starts performing the thing. If we want to think like God, then we have to go to the end first and see the completed result. We see the increase before there is any evidence of it in our lives.

Let the Holy Spirit give you vision. Visions and dreams are His language, and if you are open to Him, He will give you a vision. He's done that for me in missions many, many times. I remember once a church in Nairobi, Kenya, needed $100,000, and although I wanted to help, I really didn't see any way I could. Then the Holy Spirit in a split moment gave me a vision of Bethany giving that sum to them. Once that revelation hit, I knew it was already a fact—we were going to meet that need of the church in Kenya—and we did! Thank God for vision! Once the Lord drops the vision in your heart, then it's just a simple matter of backing up from the end and saying, "Now, Lord, I don't know how long it will take me to get to the end, but I've already seen the end from the beginning. With Your help, I'm just going to make my way there."

In the Old Testament, Joseph was a man of vision. In Genesis 41, we read of Pharaoh's dream of seven fat cows and seven lean cows. No one could interpret the dream for him, until Joseph was called from prison to do so. God gave him the interpretation of the dream: seven years of plenty to be followed by seven years of famine. Then in verses 33–36, we see how God gave Joseph a plan, or a vision, of a massive sowing and reaping effort that would bring finances and world influence to Egypt.

I think that's so interesting: Pharaoh had the dream, but Joseph got the vision! Joseph said, "Let me tell you what Pharaoh needs to do. He needs to find a wise man to supervise a massive planting program. This man should appoint officials to plant huge crops during the first seven years and store 20 percent of it for the famine that is coming. That way there will be enough for all Egypt." The massive harvest that Joseph saw coming was not for him, and he knew it. There was no way he himself could have eaten all that God was going to bring in. Joseph's vision was not for his personal success and prosperity. I think Christians ought to get delivered from that kind of thinking. God is so much bigger than you and your needs; He wants to give you a vision of conquering this world for Christ.

When you get a vision, you simply become a channel of blessing for Him. You're not meant to be a "Dead Sea," where all the blessing stops and is squandered to make yourself fatter and richer. No, you are meant to be a river of provision, flowing to bring a world harvest of souls. That was Joseph's vision. He saw a world that would perish for lack of bread unless someone had a plan. So God gave him that plan and appointed him to a position where he could carry it out.

Your expectation comes from your vision. I ask people all the time, "What is your vision?" and more times than not, I find most people, pastors included, don't have one. Or if they do have a vision, it's a very small one, like just trying to hold on to what they have, with no expectation of growth or increase. That is not vision! The vision is not, How is Aunt Susie doing this week? Is she mad at you, or is she coming to church Sunday? That is not the kind of vision God has for the local church. God wants to give the church a worldwide vision. It doesn't matter if you have only fifty people in your church—you can still have a worldwide vision. That's one thing I've learned. God gave Bethany a vision for the world when the church began in my father's living room, and forty years later we still have a vision for the world.

God gives certain vision to certain people. I don't understand everything about that, but it's true. I once heard T. L. Osborne say, "If God gives a man who is the pastor of a church a million dollar vision, then He must be intending to bless the people in the pews to fulfill that vision!" I thought about that statement and realized that if God increased my vision for world missions or any other thing, then He was going to fulfill it through the people in my church. The world isn't going to bring it to pass, but His people are the ones chosen for that privilege.

The world does not hesitate to give millions of dollars to athletes and entertainers, but I believe God desires to give millions to His people so that they can fulfill the vision of the local church. But first, you've got to start expecting it. If you're part of a local church with a large vision, just start expecting God to increase you so that you can be a part of it. Remember: Your expectation comes from your vision!

Joseph was only thirty years old when God gave him the vision, but he was quick to implement the plan God gave

The Laws of Increase

him. Verse 47 of Genesis 41 says, "And in the seven plenteous years the earth brought forth by handfuls." The harvest was by handfuls—not a little bit here and a little bit there, sweeping the floor to get a few more grains. The crops simply exploded with growth so great that Joseph couldn't keep track of it: "And Joseph gathered corn as the sand of the sea, very much, until he left numbering; for it was without number." Wouldn't it be wonderful if God poured out His blessing on you so much that you couldn't even count it? I know some of you count every penny you have, but start expecting God to increase you so that you can be a channel of His abundant blessing to a lost world.

"And all countries came into Egypt to Joseph for to buy corn; because that the famine was so sore in all lands" (Gen. 41:57). What was the purpose of God's abundant prosperity poured upon ungodly Egypt? God's purpose was to use Egypt to bless all the nations of the world. It didn't matter that Egypt didn't even serve God, for God had given Joseph a vision to bring provision for the world. "And Joseph opened all the storehouses" (v. 56). When he opened those storehouse doors, millions of dollars worth of grain came spilling out to a hungry world that couldn't provide one iota of wheat for itself. By the millions, the world came to Egypt, with sacks empty and looking for the bread that only Egypt had.

God wants His people to have storehouses of blessing, places of abundance they have reaped through intentional sowing into world missions. The storehouse is not meant to be just for us, however, but it is meant to be our source of blessing to the world. As God's people, we need to be ready to open the storehouses and provide the Bibles, tracts, TV programs, and whatever else is necessary to reach the lost.

I remember when Brother Lester Sumrall bought a huge ship in Italy and brought it to America to load it with thousands of tons of food for Liberia, where a civil war was raging at the time. When the ship reached Liberia, the starving people came by the thousands for the life-giving food. Brother Sumrall distributed the food he had brought, but he had something even greater for them. He held a huge crusade and shared the "bread of life" with them, and thousands of people were saved. He continued this ministry of providing food for hungry people, despite the criticism he received from others who couldn't understand why he would want to get involved in humanitarian aid. None of that mattered to Brother Sumrall. He had a vision from God, and He was determined to see it come to pass. That ministry continues today, even after his death in 1996.

If you are expecting increase from God so that you can bless the nations of the world, then you've got to get your storehouse ready. Deuteronomy 28:8 says, "The Lord shall command the blessing upon thee in thy storehouses, and in all that thou settest thine hand unto; and he shall bless thee in the land which the Lord thy God giveth thee." Where does it say the Lord will command the blessing upon you? In the storehouse! The storehouse is the place where you store extra things; it contains those things that are over and above your everyday amount of things. You might say, "Well, I've never had any extra, so I don't need a storehouse." If, however, you are sacrificially giving, waiting on God, and expecting increase, then it's time you built a storehouse to hold the excess that's coming. If God is going to bless your storehouse, then you'd better have one for Him to bless!

I want to challenge some of you today. Maybe you've been living from paycheck to paycheck, never having anything extra to sow as an offering in world missions or to help someone in need. By faith, start expecting your increase, and by faith, march into that bank where you do business and tell them you want to open a new account. That's going to be your storehouse, an account from which you can bless others. I don't care if you have only $5 to start with. Do it anyway, as a sign of your faith. You've got to start somewhere, and when you open that account, that is your statement of faith that you believe God is going to increase you. So get ready for it!

As God begins blessing you, first place within your storehouse enough to cover several months' living expenses in case of emergency. Some of you are saying right about now, "Oh, Pastor, I don't know if God can do that for me. I can never put more than $2 worth of gas in my car at a time, and I'm always juggling my bills just to try to get everybody paid. I can't even imagine ever having extra for myself, let alone others." God is so much bigger than you are, and as you are faithful to manage what resources you do have, God will give you more so that you can put it in your storehouse. Every month, start putting something in your storehouse. Be consistent in it, and begin to believe God. He's going to bless your storehouse!

In 2 Chronicles 31, Hezekiah instructed the people to bring in their tithes and offerings, and verse 5 records their response: "And as soon as the commandment came abroad, the children of Israel brought in abundance the firstfruits of corn, wine, and oil, and honey, and of all the increase of the field; and the tithe of all things brought they in abundantly." They had abundance, and they delighted in giving it to the house of the Lord. In fact, they had so much to give that they "laid them by heaps" (v. 6). I like that—God's people had so much to give that it was heaped into great big piles! There was no lack, no stinginess, no need for anyone to hold back.

When Hezekiah saw this generous response on the part of the people, he questioned Azariah, chief priest of the house of Zadok about it. Azariah told him, "Since the people began to bring the offerings into the house of the Lord, we have had enough to eat, and have left plenty: for the Lord hath blessed his people; and that which is left is this great store" (v. 10). Once the people started giving their offerings to the Lord, the blessing of God simply overtook them. They had plenty for themselves and plenty left over. That's how it can be for you, too. Once you begin to tithe and give offerings, the laws of increase begin working on your behalf, and you'll have enough for you and plenty left over to put into your storehouse to bless others.

That's what Hezekiah did with the increase. He ordered chambers to be built in the house of the Lord to contain the overflowing abundance. In the Hebrew, the word for *chamber* is "storehouse"; thus, Hezekiah had storehouses built to hold the increase. God wants to give you a storehouse. It's time to think beyond "me, my wife, our two kids: us four and no more." That's not enough for God's people. He does want you to have enough for your family, but He wants to give you plenty left over to bless others, too. The day of "gimme, gimme, my name is Jimmy" is over! You're not meant to be always looking at how you can get a little bit more here and there. No, that's not good enough for a child of God. God is a God of increase, and He wants that for you.

Start with the tithe, and then move on to giving offerings. Don't let the devil keep stealing your increase from you. He's told some of you, "Your daddy was poor, your granddaddy was poor, and you're going to be poor, too." When that kind of thought comes into your mind, just rise up and say, "No, I am blessed. I will have storehouses. I will have such an abundance that I can give to the nations of the world." Then kick the devil out and get your storehouse ready!

I would love to see God's people so prosperous and sowing so much into the Lord's work that not one missionary would ever have to go without. From my years as a missionary in Nigeria, I know what it's like to have a vehicle that you have to push more than you can drive. I remember trying desperately to keep my vehicle running, pouring in the brake fluid every few days and literally using baling wire to hold the carburetor together. I don't want any missionary to have to live like that. That's why I'm expecting God to bless and increase you so that you, in turn, can be a blessing to missionaries all over the world. I've had enough of little tiny visions that just hope to have enough to make it through the day. I want a big vision—with heaps of blessing and storehouses overflowing to the world.

Expect to receive seed!

After God has given you vision, the next step is to expect to receive seed. When you build your storehouse, you're looking at the vision God gave you and getting ready for it to come to pass. Once the storehouse is in place, you need the seed to plant so you can reap a harvest to fill the storehouse. You're responsible for setting up the storehouse, but God is responsible for giving you the seed for it. Look what 2 Corinthians 9:10 NIV says: "Now *he who supplies seed to the sower* and bread for food *will also supply and increase your store of seed* and will enlarge the harvest of your righteousness" (italics added). God is the one responsible for supplying you with seed! That's a beautiful principle that takes all the pressure off you and puts it on God. If you are faithful, if you are a good steward of what you have, and if you get your storehouse ready, God will give you the seed. That's what the Word of God says.

The real issue is not whether or not God will give you seed—He will do that—but what you will do with the seed when He gives it. Will you sow into world missions, or will you yield to the desire to keep it for yourself and, in effect, eat your seed? Be on the lookout for seed; expect it to come. But when it does, don't say, "Oh, good, now I can buy that new TV I've been wanting." Recognize the seed as God's opportunity to you to sow to a harvest of souls.

Notice that I said sow *to* a harvest. So many people think that they should sow *from* a harvest, that is, after they have abundance, but I've learned that's not the way it works. Farmers know that, and we have to learn that, too. When farmers have had their crops fail, the next year they have to sow more seed towards the harvest they're expecting. So the fact that you have nothing right now does not mean you don't sow. Ask God to give you the seed to sow and be on the lookout for it. Plant that seed *to* the harvest you're expecting.

God's seed to you is always legitimate seed. He is never going to give you dishonest seed that belongs to someone else. It's like a woman who came up to me one time to tell me how God how "blessed" her. She went to an ATM machine and it started spitting out bills. She was so excited that God had "provided," but of course, I instructed her that the money was not hers, but belonged to the bank. God will never provide for you in that way.

Keep your integrity intact while you're looking for your seed. Don't get goofy and see spiritual significance where common sense can tell you right from wrong. One time I bought my wife, Melanie, a CD player. We were in the store looking at it, and the salesman put in a Christmas CD so we could hear the quality of the sound. We decided to buy the CD player and were talking with the clerk, not paying much attention. When we got to the car, we were looking at our purchase and noticed the clerk had left the CD in the player. Was that God "blessing" me so I could give the CD to someone for Christmas? Of course not! I knew that, and you would, too. So Melanie and I got out of the car, trudged across the parking lot, went into the mall, walked into the store where we had bought the CD player, rode the escalator into the right department, and went up to the man who had sold it to us. We handed the CD over to him, saying, "Sir, I believe this belongs to you." That clerk was so grateful. He had noticed the CD was missing and was already concerned that he was going to have to pay for it. But we knew God never gives to us in a dishonest fashion. If it doesn't belong to you or wasn't given to you honestly, then it's not seed—

The Laws of Increase

no matter what the devil may try to tell you.

God does give seed, however, and many times He gives from unexpected sources. I remember a story the late John Osteen of Lakewood Church told me one time. He said that he had recently gotten a letter from a woman in his church who had been a maid for a wealthy family. She was sent to do some shopping for them and was told to buy herself lunch with whatever money was left over. The maid did as she was instructed, but after purchasing the items, she had no money left for lunch. That day it seemed she was particularly hungry. She so much wanted something to eat, but she didn't have any money left over.

As the woman walked to her car, she saw something green on the ground and reached down and picked it up. It was a $10 bill, and there was no way to tell where it had come from or to whom it belonged. So she picked up the money and began rejoicing that God had provided her with money for lunch. She began to go back inside the mall to get something to eat when all of a sudden she remembered that she had just recently told the Lord that if she ever found any money, she would regard it as seed and sow it into world missions.

The woman faced a struggle at this point, but she was faithful, and said, "Well, Lord, I want to be faithful to you. This is seed you have provided that I might be blessed and be a blessing. I'll sow it into world missions." She put her hunger on hold, got into the car, went home, and ate some soup and crackers. She kept her word and gave the money to missions.

Several weeks later, Brother Osteen told me, this woman inherited a vast fortune so large that she would never have to

The Laws of Increase

work another day in her life. I wonder what would have happened if she had eaten her seed instead of sowing it like she had promised? I'm not saying we are all going to become millionaires, but I'm making the point that you've got to recognize your seed when it comes, be faithful to sow it, and then watch God multiply it.

God wants to increase your supply of seed. His blessing is not a one-time thing. He wants to keep on giving you seed so you can keep on sowing into world missions and He can keep on reaping a harvest back to you. He wants the cycle to go on and on. But if you consume the seed rather than planting it, you stop the entire cycle of blessing.

It's sort of like priming a pump. If you never pour any water down the well, you can pump all you want, but nothing is going to come up. There's water down there, but you're not going to get the benefit of it because you haven't primed the pump. God is going to give you seed. He'll give you a little at first to see if you'll be faithful with it. You might be tempted to say, "Lord, I'm so thirsty; I want to drink this water so bad." But go ahead and pour it down the well, and watch the river that comes flowing out of it to you! That's all God is really looking for. He wants to bless you, but He's got to see if you'll be faithful. He wants to see if you'll receive seed as something to sow into the harvest fields of the world or if you just see it as something to meet your needs.

Expect a harvest!

As you are learning to expect increase from God, you first expect vision. Next, you expect seed. Finally, you expect the harvest. You must be fully persuaded that the God who gave you the vision and the seed to sow toward it is true to His Word and will come through for you.

Look at this verse in 1 Corinthians 9:10: "He that ploweth should plow in hope; and that he that thresheth in hope should be partaker of his hope." The Amplified Bible says it like this: "The plowman ought to plow in hope, and the thresher ought to thresh in expectation of partaking of the harvest." That means we're to always be looking around every corner for our harvest. We're to never lose hope and never despair. Don't go around saying, "I'll be like this the rest of my life. I have no hope of ever increasing." No, see yourself blessed with God's abundance. See yourself blessed as a soul-winner. See that fractured relationship mended. If you've been faithfully sowing your seed, then expect your harvest to come.

Receive the vision from God, get your storehouse ready, plant to the size of your vision, be constantly on the lookout for seed to sow, and then be faithful to plant it when it comes. If you're doing all these things, God's law of reciprocity will kick in, and your harvest will come. Luke 6:27–38 has quite a bit to say on this subject. Throughout this passage, Jesus is teaching the principle of reaping what you sow. That's why He gives so many admonitions to take care how you sow. In verse 27 Jesus said, "Love your enemies." The world says to get even with your enemies, but Jesus says to love them. When you do, you're planting a seed of love that you can expect a return on.

Verses 10–11 continue with "do good to them that hate you, bless them that curse you, and pray for them which despitefully use you." What are you going to do if someone curses you? You're going to speak words of blessing over that person and plant a seed in his life. Furthermore, you're going to pray for those who take advantage of you.

The instruction goes on, seeming even more far-fetched: "And unto him that smiteth thee on the one cheek offer also the other; and him that taketh away thy cloak forbid not to take thy coat also. Give to every man that asketh of thee; and of him that taketh away thy goods ask them not again" (vv. 29–30). These are serious words the Lord is speaking to us, but He knows we'll reap a mighty harvest of righteousness if we will live by them.

Years ago I learned that nobody can rip me off, because if someone takes something from me, I just release it as a seed and God multiplies it back to me. Now, don't misunderstand me: I don't try to intentionally get taken advantage of. I don't leave my car running at the mall, and I don't leave my possessions strewn all over my front lawn. But if someone does take something from me, I don't worry about it and fuss and fume. I just release it and let the Lord take care of it.

If somebody talks behind your back and takes your job from you, so what? Pray for those who despitefully use you. "But love ye your enemies, and do good, and lend, hoping for nothing again; and your reward shall be great, and ye shall be the children of the Highest: for he is kind unto the unthankful and to the evil" (v. 35). When you love the unlovely and do good with no ulterior motive, you're acting like your heavenly Father. He will reward you greatly for the seeds of love you sow to those who don't deserve it.

The verses roll on, telling us to show mercy (v. 36), not to judge and condemn (v. 37), and to forgive (v. 37). Forgive—that, perhaps, is the hardest thing to do. When someone has hurt us deeply, the natural tendency is to hold on to that hurt and to hold it against the one who did it. All of us have been wounded at some time or another by someone we loved. But if we will forgive, releasing that hurt and planting it as a seed, the Lord will bless us for it.

A few years back, I received a letter from a lady in our congregation that beautifully brought this point home. One day her husband came home and announced that he was leaving her. He did just that, leaving her in a trailer with no money, no job, and children to take care of. She and her children were so hurt; their world had been turned upside down in just a moment's time.

This woman lived about forty minutes away from the church, and after her husband abandoned her, she had no way to get to church. When her cell group heard what had happened, they rallied behind her and got to work. They pooled their money and collected enough to move her trailer closer to the church. Then her zone pastor and some other men built a porch for her, installed skirting around the trailer, and hooked up all the plumbing and electricity for her. Then a woman in the cell group took the lady's children into her own home for two weeks so that their mother would be free to go out and look for a job.

Because of the actions of all these people, the woman wrote me, saying, "I have never experienced such love. These people moved my trailer, helped me get set up, and helped me get a job. We live right across the street from the church now—we could even walk to church if we had to—but God made it possible for me to buy a car. I have forgiven my husband, and I am blessed!" This woman had every right to get angry and bitter at her husband, but she refused. She released him to the Lord, and God took that seed of forgiveness and sowed it back to her, meeting all her needs in the process.

Get a vision from God, prepare your storehouse to contain the blessing, watch for God to give you seed to sow, and then make sure to plant the seed He gives you. After you've done all that, you can expect God's laws of increase to begin working for you. If you need love, sow love into the life of someone else. Show mercy to others, and you will receive mercy. Give forgiveness, and you're granted forgiveness. That's how it works in the kingdom of God. What are you expecting to receive from God? Sow that very thing into the life of another.

Finally, in verse 38 we come to the end of Jesus' discourse: "Give and it shall be given unto you." That's the reciprocal nature of the laws of increase at work. You give, and it is given to you. You can't stop it, and you can't outrun God's blessings. It's a law of the Spirit, and it will happen if you expect it. The verse goes on: ". . . good measure, pressed down, shaken together, and running over shall men give into your bosom." God's blessings aren't stingy—they're the "running over" kind! Have you ever pushed your foot down into a trash can, pressing down all the trash so that you could fit more into it? That's what you call "pressed down." Then you shake the can around a little to make everything settle so you can squeeze just a little bit more in. That's "shaken together." By the time you're through, that trash can is "running over." It's so full, you can hardly get it out to the curb.

That's the way God's blessings are. He presses and shakes and brings so much more into your life that you can hardly contain it. When He says that "men will give into your bosom," He's talking about your lap. The Jewish people wore long, flowing garments, and when they needed to carry something, they would make a fold in the garment and hold it out in front of them. Then they would receive the grain or whatever else they needed, tying a knot in the garment to secure it. You have a "Holy Ghost garment." Open up that big apron you have, hold it out in front of you, and let God fill it to overflowing. "For with the same measure that you mete, withal it shall be measured to you again" (v. 38).

I want to live in the Father's abundance. I don't want to lack, never able to help anybody or to sow into world missions. I'm going to keep on giving my tithe, keep on giving offerings, continue waiting for God, and I'm going to expect Him to pour me out a blessing so large that I can't contain it. How about you?

CHAPTER 5

Receiving Your Increase

Finally, in this chapter we come to the last of the five laws of increase. In our acronym of SOWER, we learned that "S" stands for sacrifice; "O," for offerings; "W," for waiting; "E," for expectation; and the "R," as we'll see in this chapter, stands for receiving. If you understand the first four laws of increase but fail to grasp the fifth and final law, then the blessing God wants to give you will always lie just beyond your reach. It's critical that you learn how to *receive* your increase.

For some of us, receiving is a hard thing. We value our independence and don't want to receive anything from anybody. We want to take care of ourselves. To a degree, that's good. We shouldn't be lying around wanting whatever we can get from whoever will give it to us. That's lazy and selfish. However, there is a time and a place for receiving.

Most of us are used to small, limited thinking. Somehow we think that if God blesses us, there won't be enough for someone else who "really needs it." God, however, is limitless in His resources. When He gives to you, He is not diminished in any way. He's got so much more than you could ever imagine. There is plenty for all His children.

Some people have real needs, but for some reason, they think it's spiritual to not ask for too much or expect God to give too much. They might need a car and pray for one, but they say things like, "Lord, please bless me with a car. Any old one will do. I don't want to be greedy, Lord. As long as it works most of the time, that's okay with me." God deliver us from that kind of thinking! Like a loving father, God wants you to have what you need. He's just waiting for you to be able to receive it.

In Genesis 12:3, God told Abraham that He would make him great—that he would be blessed so that through him all the nations of the world could be blessed. Abraham knew that he could never *be* a blessing unless he first *received* a blessing from God. You've got to know that, too. So get rid of that old "poor me" mentality and begin to receive from the Lord. Get rid of that old "I'll be broke all my life" mentality and open your storehouse unto the Lord. Throw out that old "I'll never win souls" mentality and begin to receive the anointing of a soul-winner. You must be blessed in order to bless—it's that simple.

So many people don't know how to receive. It's sort of like having a radio station in town with a big tower to transmit, but never turning on your radio to receive the programming. You can talk about the radio station all you want—how incompetent it is, how weak the signal is, or any other excuse—but the real problem is that your switch is turned off. It's impossible for you to receive until you actually turn your radio on.

You've probably been around teenagers who had headphones on, enjoying music that only they could hear. You had no idea what they were listening to because you couldn't hear it, but they had their receiver on and they were enjoying it! It's like that in the house of God. Some of you go to church every week, sitting in the same pew near the same people. But you've noticed that they seem to be receiving something that you're not. They're getting excited and "amen-ing" the preacher, and you're looking at your watch, wondering what time you're going to get out of there. Brother, turn your receiver on!

You've got to have a receiving mentality and an abiding faith that your heavenly Father is waiting to bless you. Look at Luke 11:13: "If ye then, being evil, know how to give good gifts unto your children: how much more shall your heavenly Father give the Holy Spirit to them that ask him?" If you, as an earthly parent, know how to give good things to your children, don't you think the heavenly Father knows how to bless you? He's got a few surprises in store for you; He hasn't told you everything He's planned. He's just waiting for the right time to shower His gifts upon you.

When my two youngest sons, James and Jason, were toddlers, my wife and I took them to a local toy store around Christmastime so that we could buy their Christmas presents. They ran over to this toy and then ran over to that one. They were so excited with everything that they could hardly contain themselves. My wife and I just walked along behind them with a shopping cart, and whenever we noticed an extra loud squeal of delight, we knew we had found something they really liked. The boys would run on, and we would pitch that thing into the basket, then continue strolling along behind them. They never realized that we were watching them and picking out wonderful gifts to bless them with on Christmas morning.

God knows how to bless you, just like my wife and I knew how to bless our little boys. We had so much fun buying gifts for them, and God delights to have gifts in store for you, too. So stop trying to figure everything out. Some of you torment yourself with endless questions that go nowhere: When is my boss going to give me a raise? . . . I bet he doesn't even like me . . . Probably everybody else except me will get a bonus . . . and on the list goes. Stop that whining! Your boss is not your source; you serve God and He'll take care of you. And just about the time you think God hasn't heard your prayer, if you'll turn around, you'll see Him putting it in the shopping cart!

If you back up to verse 10 in Luke 13, there is another interesting statement: "For every one that asketh receiveth; and he that seeketh findeth; and to him that knocketh it shall be opened." The Father wants you to ask, and then He wants you to receive what you asked for. His ears are open to you; He is looking and listening for the little hints you drop of the things you desire. Your heart's desire is so special to God. It truly is!

I once read about the famous missionary evangelist Dr. John Lake, who as a young boy went into an executive's office in Chicago and saw a beautiful mahogany desk with ivory inlay. That day he thought to himself, "One day I'm going to have a desk like that." Life went on, and he forgot all about the incident. He grew up and went into the insurance business. God blessed as he tithed and gave offerings, and John Lake became the wealthy CEO of a large insurance company. One year the company gave him a gift—a large mahogany desk with ivory inlay. At that moment, the Lord brought back to his mind the unspoken desire of his heart as a teenager, and Lake realized the Lord had brought it to pass.

We all have to learn this lesson of asking and receiving. Most of you have probably heard of Dr. Cho of Korea. In 1957 he was not yet well known; in fact, he was a poverty-stricken pastor in Seoul, meeting in the slums of the city in a leftover American tent from the Korean War. Furthermore, he had no transportation to enable him to visit his parishioners. He began praying generally for a bicycle until one day he sensed the Lord asking him, "What kind of bike?"

He quickly answered, "Lord, it doesn't matter; any kind of bicycle will do."

The Lord replied, "Until you get specific with Me, I'm not going to give you what you want. I don't know your heart's desire."

Pastor Cho proceeded to write down exactly the kind of bike he wanted: a red bike like the American GIs rode. Within a month, he was provided with the exact kind of bike he had prayed for. From this experience, Dr. Cho learned to make known to God the desires of his heart, to ask specifically for them, and then to receive them from the hand of the Father.

Psalm 37:4 says, "Delight yourself also in the Lord, and

He shall give you the desires of your heart." When you are enjoying God and serving Him from your heart, then you will ask for things from right motives. James 4:3 says that many times we ask and don't receive because we are motivated by wrong reasons. If you are full of greed, envy, or pride, God is not going to be able to bless you with the desires of your heart. If, on the other hand, you remain humble and childlike in your relationship with the Lord, then He simply can't wait to bless you and give you your heart's desire.

You must conceive before you can receive!

In the first chapter of Luke, we can read contrasting stories of two different people: one who was unable to receive from God and one who could. These two people, Zacharias and Mary, represent the two opposing ways of responding when God speaks a word to bless you. In verse 13 of this chapter, the angel Gabriel appeared to Zacharias and proceeded to tell him that God was going to give him and his barren wife a very special son. Zacharias and his wife were advanced in age, physically unable to have the child they had desired for so many years. Now suddenly, an angel of the Lord says, "Fear not, Zacharias: for thy prayer is heard; and thy wife Elisabeth shall bear thee a son, and thou shalt call his name John."

You would think that Zacharias would have immediately begun shouting and dancing all around the temple. Finally, his deepest desire was going to be fulfilled—he and Elizabeth were going to have a son! Maybe it had been so long that Zacharias couldn't believe anymore, or maybe the knowledge of his wife's advanced age discouraged him, but for whatever reason, Zacharias couldn't receive the joyous words of the angel. He doubted and expressed his unbelief to the angel: "Whereby shall I know this? For I am an old man, and my wife well stricken in years" (v. 18).

The angel then answered, "And, behold, thou shalt be dumb, and not able to speak, until the day that these things shall be performed, because thou believest not my words, which shall be fulfilled in their season" (v. 20). In other words, it was like God was saying, "If you're not going to believe it, I'll do it anyway, but you're going to pay a price for your unbelief." Zacharias, from that moment on until the birth of his son, John the Baptist, was unable to speak. Elizabeth, true to the word of the angel, conceived in her old age and went into seclusion for five months.

In Elizabeth's sixth month of pregnancy, the crowning moment of all human history came to pass. God again sent Gabriel to the earth, with a message of such magnitude as to be unbelievable to the natural human heart. God had been waiting four thousand years to deliver that glorious word of redemption, and when the precise moment came, He turned to Gabriel and said, "It's time, Gabriel. Deliver the word to the little maiden named Mary."

I can just imagine it. The mighty Gabriel sent from the very throne of almighty God to a young, unknown virgin girl of Israel! There was little Mary—probably washing dishes or baking bread—just going about her business as she had done every day of her young life. There was nothing to indicate this day would be any different from any other,

The Laws of Increase

but all of a sudden Mary looked up, and there was this awesome being before her.

Then Gabriel spoke: "Hail, thou that art highly favoured, the Lord is with thee: blessed art thou among women" (v. 28). Gabriel continued, unfolding the vision and painting it on the canvas of Mary's heart: "And, behold, thou shalt conceive in thy womb, and bring forth a son, and shalt call his name Jesus. He shall be great, and shall be called the Son of the Highest: and the Lord God shall give unto him the throne of his father David: And he shall reign over the house of Jacob for ever; and of his kingdom there shall be no end" (vv. 31–33).

What a glorious day, not only for Mary, but also for all humanity for all time! In a crude dwelling in Nazareth, a virgin girl suddenly found herself in the midst of God's eternal plan. There was Gabriel, imparting the vision to her heart with one mighty paint stroke after another: "You shall conceive . . . Your son will be great . . . God will give him a throne . . . He'll reign forever and ever." By the time Gabriel was finished, that vision was emblazoned on Mary's heart. She saw it! Even though not one bit of it had happened yet, she saw it clearly with the eyes of faith.

Brothers and sisters, you've got to get a vision. You've got to conceive it deep down in your heart where it's as real as anything you see in the natural world. If you don't have a vision, you're spiritually dead. You're spiritually blind, unable to see what God has called you to do or the many blessings of increase He has waiting for you. If you have not conceived in your heart a vision from God, you'll have no joy. Vision is your very source of joy! When you conceive

The Laws of Increase

something by faith, you receive it in your heart, but if you never receive it in the spiritual, you'll never see it in the natural. Until that vision drops from your head to your heart, you'll never be able to receive it and God cannot give it to you.

So Mary saw the vision. She embraced it in her heart, but she had a question about it: "How shall this be, seeing I know not a man?" (v. 34). Notice the difference between her question and Zacharias's. Zacharias said, "Whereby shall I know?" Mary, on the other hand, asked, "How shall this be?" Zacharias didn't *know* that it could be; he had not conceived the vision in his heart. Mary, however, said, "It *shall* be; I just don't know how because I am a virgin." Zacharias's question had to do with rationality, but Mary's dealt with chastity. She was simply asking how she was going to remain moral and yet conceive.

Verse 35 records the answer: "The Holy Ghost shall come upon thee, and the power of the Highest shall overshadow thee." The Holy Ghost—how I love those three words! Anything you are going to receive from God is first conceived in your heart through the power of the Holy Ghost. Only then can it be birthed in the natural. It doesn't matter how impossible the vision seems; if it is conceived by the Holy Ghost, it will come to pass. It's like what Zechariah in the Old Testament was told: "Not by might, nor by power, but by my spirit" (Zech. 4:6).

With the Holy Spirit, the vision and its fulfillment are a "done deal." Verse 37 in Luke 1 declares, "For with God nothing shall be impossible." No vision is too big, too expensive, or too unusual for God to fulfill, but before you

The Laws of Increase

can see it come to pass, you must first see it in your heart. You have to see the vision in its final form before you can ever see its beginning. If you need healing in your body, you must see with the eyes of your spirit the day when you are well. If you're scrounging around trying to make ends meet, you've got to see the day when your bills are paid and you have money left over to sow into the nations of the world. God is there wanting to increase you, but your "receiver" isn't turned on. He's beaming the signal, but you've got to be able to receive it.

I think about the widow in the Old Testament in 2 Kings 4. Her husband had died, and she was left alone with her two sons. She owed money to creditors, and one day they came to collect. In those days if you couldn't pay a debt, you or a family member was forced into slavery to work it off. The widow went to Elisha for help, and he asked her what she had in the house. All she had was a little oil. He told her to collect vessels from her neighbors, go into her house and shut the door, and then pour the oil she had into the vessels. She sent her boys out into the neighborhood to get the vessels, and when they returned, the three of them went into the house and filled every one of those vessels from the little cruse of oil. The oil never stopped flowing until she ran out of vessels.

That widow received the vision in her heart when all she had was a small bottle of oil in the house. But she turned her receiver on and did what Elisha told her to do. I can just see her pouring oil into the first vessel. Then she filled another . . . and another . . . and another. She just kept pouring because the vision was in her heart. She had tapped into a source much bigger than she was—a source with more oil than the Alaskan pipeline!

The Holy Spirit has such big plans and vision for your life, if you will only turn on your receiver and pick up His signal. I knew a young man who did just that and let God give him a creative idea of increase. This man had the idea to create a special kind of bag to hold toxic waste. It's not very exciting, is it? Just a bag, but it was something that was needed. So the man formed a company and began producing this bag. He was a faithful brother and a faithful tither in his church. As God blessed him, he gave more and more to the Lord's work. He told the Lord, "I just want to be a clear channel for you to use." One year he told the Lord, "If you'll bless me with a profit of $300,000, I will not only tithe on it but also give missionary offerings." That year he cleared $300,000 and, true to his word, tithed and gave offerings. All from the vision of a little bag that the Holy Spirit planted in his heart!

When God finds a clean, clear channel—someone who's ready to receive and has the vessels waiting—He'll pour the oil in until there are no more vessels. The question is not, Does God have enough? but the real question is, Do you have your vessels ready?

In 2 Kings 3, Israel was facing a battle but had no water for their men or animals. The need for water was desperate, so they called for the prophet Elisha. In verse 16, Elisha told them, "Make this valley full of ditches." Now that is not really the word you're looking for from a prophet. The men were probably grumbling and complaining, but they, nevertheless, obeyed Elisha's word and dug ditches. That's usually

The Laws of Increase

the way God does things: He makes you dig a ditch before He fills it with water. That's what Israel and Judah had to do. The next morning when they arose, those ditches were filled with water. It had not rained during the night, but the ditches were miraculously full. Moab, their enemy, saw the sun reflecting off the water and thought it was blood. Thinking the Israelites had killed one another, Moab attacked, only to be cut down by Israel. Brother, get your shovel and start digging your ditch! Get the vision in your heart and then anticipate its coming. God is sending the water!

When God gives a vision, your mind must be stretched to receive the impossible. For Mary, the thought of her becoming pregnant without having relations was absurd, in the natural. However, look at what she said in Luke 1:38: "Behold the handmaid of the Lord; be it unto me according to thy word." The word of God spoken to your heart will always bear fruit, just like the word of God spoken to Mary came to pass. She didn't understand it—she just surrendered to the will of God and received it. She conceived that vision in her heart, and then it was conceived in her body.

You've got to change the way you've been thinking about God's blessings. He is not limited by what you think is possible; He's so much bigger than that. Look in Jeremiah 33:3: "Call unto me, and I will answer thee, and show thee great and mighty things, which thou knowest not." You don't even know the great and mighty things the Lord has in store for you! But He said that if you would call to Him, He'd answer. If you have no vision, I challenge you to pray, to call upon the name of the Lord and ask Him what great and mighty things He has for you. Stretch your mind and your faith, and wait to see what He will tell you. Dare to ask Him for seed, more than you think is possible. It has nothing to do with you and your abilities, but everything to do with who He is.

A chapter earlier in Jeremiah 32, verses 17 and 18, the prophet gives an awesome description of who God is: "Ah Lord God! Behold, thou hast made the heaven and the earth by thy great power and stretched out arm, and there is nothing too hard for thee. . . . the Great, the Mighty God, the Lord of hosts, is his name." Verse 19 tells us what He is great in: "Great in counsel, and mighty in work." Do you need counsel? God has the perfect counsel for any situation, and He will give it to you when you call upon Him. He's mighty in works, too. He's not just so-so, doing a little of this and a little of that—He's mighty! That means He's all-powerful; there's nothing He can't do. Can He pay off your house for you? Yes! Can He bless you financially so that you have money left over to sow into world missions? Yes! Can He give you souls for His kingdom! A thousand times, yes! Can He heal your body or restore your mind or mend your marriage? Yes, yes, yes! The Great and Mighty One reigns!

Back in verse 3 of Jeremiah 33, God told us that He would show us great and mighty things. He goes on to list some of them: physical healing (v. 6), prosperity (v. 9), and joy (vv. 11–14). He is waiting to reveal those things to those who ask. Verse 6 says, "I will bring it health and cure, and I will cure them." The Great and Mighty One wants to heal your body. He's big enough to restore organs that have failed, to sweep away death from a cancer-ravaged body, and to deliver the troubled mind tormented by demons.

Many, many people have gotten that vision of a great big God who heals their bodies and are walking proofs of the God who still does miracles. If you need healing, turn on your receiver today, call on your God, and receive the mighty work He wants to do in you.

Verse 9 says, "... They shall fear and tremble for all the goodness and for all the prosperity that I procure unto it." When the Bible talks about God's prosperity, it's not talking about His lavishing on you all kinds of stuff just so you can be boastful and haughty. It's nothing but foolishness to think God is going to bless you just so you can think you're "all that." Pride never has a place in the kingdom of God.

But He does want to bless you so that the unbelieving nations of the world can see the prosperity He pours out upon His people. It brings no glory to God for you to never have enough. It does not honor Him in the sight of your relatives if you're always begging and borrowing from them. His desire is to financially bless you so that when the sinner looks at you, he'll say, "My, my, my! What has happened to you? Everything you touch just turns to gold, and every time I see you, you have more and more."

When you start applying the laws of increase, you can't help but grow. One year you're cutting your lawn with a weed eater, and next year you move up to a push mower. Then you get a little riding lawn mower, and before you know it, you've got a tractor to mow your grass! In the meantime, your neighbor across the street is still using a weed eater to cut his grass, wondering all the time why you keep increasing. You can go ahead and keep using that weed eater if you want, but as for me, I'm looking for that tractor with my name on it. I want all the blessing and bounty the Great and Mighty One has for me. And when those blessings start rolling into my life, I'm going to turn around and sow them right back into the kingdom of God. That, my friend, is true prosperity.

Be it done . . . according to your word.

When Gabriel appeared to Mary with the vision of God for her life, Mary received what she heard and the vision was conceived, quite literally, within her. That's the way it works. The Holy Spirit gives the vision, but we have to decide whether or not we will embrace it and believe it.

Receiving faith rests strictly upon the promises of the Word of God. It does not need to see anything change in the natural world before it will believe. It receives the promise, and the promise represents the reality that is yet to come.

Jesus knew how critical it was for us to know how to receive. Remember the story of blind Bartimaeus in Mark 10:46–52? When Bartimaeus heard that Jesus was passing by, he received the vision in his heart that Jesus could give him physical sight. He began to call out to Him, pleading for mercy. No amount of shushing from anyone around him could deter Bartimaeus from petitioning the Lord for his sight. He already knew that Jesus could do it; it was just a matter of receiving it from Him.

Attentive to the cries of Bartimaeus, Jesus called him to Him and asked what seemed to be a ridiculous question: "What wilt thou that I should do unto thee?" (v. 51). In other words, Jesus said, "What do you want, Bartimaeus?" What a question! Wasn't it obvious? The man was blind and probably needed help every day of his life, and now Jesus was asking, "What do you want?" Humbly Bartimaeus replied, "Lord, that I might *receive* my sight" (v. 51, italics added). It was time for Bartimaeus to receive. The moment had come, and Bartimaeus, grasping the opportunity, received in his body what he had already received in his heart. His eyes were opened, and he followed Jesus.

What do *you* want? Like Bartimaeus, what is the one thing you desperately need from the Lord? He's asking you that question today, right now: What do you want? See it in your spirit, and then receive it in manifested form.

Jesus taught us to receive the promise of whatever we asked for in prayer. In Mark 11, the Bible records the story of Jesus' cursing of the fig tree that had no fruit on it. The next day, as they were passing the tree, the disciples saw that it had withered and died. Remembering the previous day's events, they were amazed, and Peter commented on it to Jesus. Jesus exhorted them to "have faith in God" (v. 22) and then in verses 23–24, He spoke the keys to receiving:

> For verily I say unto you, That whosoever shall say unto this mountain, Be thou removed, and be thou cast into the sea; and shall not doubt in his heart, but shall believe that those things which he saith shall come to pass; he shall have whatsoever he saith. [24]Therefore I say unto you, What things soever ye desire, when ye pray, believe that ye receive them, and ye shall have them.

God is looking at your heart's desire, and when your

heart's desire is aligned with His desire, you can pray in confidence that He will answer. If your heart is pure, full of right motives, and passionate for the lost of this world, God will delight to bless you with increase. If you are praying, "Lord, supply me with seed to sow. I want to be a blessing to others. I want to be a part of this final end-time harvest," then God will move heaven and earth to accomplish His blessing in your life.

I like the way the NIV phrases verse 24: "Therefore I tell you, whatever you ask for in prayer, believe that you have received it, and it will be yours." That's the crux of the problem for some of you; you've been saying, "I believe I *will* receive," but God is waiting for you to realize that you already *have* received! Isn't that what the Word of God says? The word *will* speaks of the future, of something that hasn't happened yet, but the words *have received* speak of a past action. That's a vital difference to understand.

I can just hear some of you thinking: "Now, Brother Larry, let's not get out there on the edge somewhere. Let's use common sense." But, brother, I challenge you to go right on out to the edge of the water and then walk on it! That's what Peter did, and that's what I'm going to do, too. I'm going to believe that I have already received whatever I am praying for. Then it's just a matter of time before I see it come to pass.

There shall be a performance of those things which were told. . . .

When Mary visited Elizabeth, her cousin immediately

The Laws of Increase

recognized the significance of what had happened to Mary. Speaking to Mary, she declared, "Blessed is she that believed: for there shall be a performance of those things which were told her from the Lord" (Luke 1:45). First, Mary had to believe the unbelievable proclamation from Gabriel, and then it was effected within her body. The Scripture does not record the exact moment when the Holy Spirit came upon her, but when she humbly said, "Behold the handmaid of the Lord; be it unto me according to thy word" (v. 38), she demonstrated her acceptance and belief in the plan of God.

Maybe it happened then or maybe it was that evening, but whenever it occurred, I believe the Holy Spirit filled that room with the glory of God. The Holy Spirit of God enveloped that receptive little virgin, and deep within her womb was planted the seed of God. What a holy, holy thought and moment! That little seed, divine yet human, came into contact with Mary's egg. Since the bloodline was carried through the male's seed, this life in Mary's womb would not be tainted by the blood of man, but instead would come into the world, spotless and clean—the Son of God Himself.

As that peasant girl stood there, overcome by the presence of God, she conceived the Savior of the world. She may not have felt any different, but in faith she had conceived the vision from God and immediately went to visit Elizabeth. Together they rejoiced at the great and awesome works of God.

Just like the Holy Spirit did with Mary, He wants to implant vision in your heart. He wants to give you the picture of blessing and increase. He wants you to become pregnant with the vision. Conceive it in your heart, and then carry that vision full-term. Believe that God has blessed you so that you can be a blessing to others. See yourself overflowing with abundance and being used as a channel of blessing. God fully intends to perform what He has promised you, but you have to carry the vision to term, not aborting it or causing it to miscarry in your life.

Mary, after conceiving Jesus, went with haste to Judea, eager to share her news with Elizabeth. She fellowshipped with those who had the same vision and faith. They worshipped God together, shouted together, and rejoiced together. When you are pregnant with vision, pass the time of your "pregnancy" with those of like faith. In that way, your vision will be delivered right on time.

Never give up on the vision of increase God has given you. Once you grasp it in your heart, make provision for it in your life. Commit today to being a sower in the kingdom of God. Give the sacrifice of the tithe. Present offerings to the work of the Lord around the world. Wait on God to bring the increase, and expect to see it. Finally, receive the increase in your heart that it might be manifested in your life.

The infinite God of the universe is waiting on you. He wants to bless. He wants to grant your heart's desire. He wants to see you victorious and walking in abundance in the laws of increase. His will, without a doubt, is to increase you more and more!